A Frost In Hell

The True Story of
The Petersham Butcher of 1875

Doug 'VB' Goudie

To my wife's brother Bobby,
a man who proves that not all brothers-in-law
need to be killed.

Contents

Introduction

I grew up in the small town of Petersham, Massachusetts. It is one of only three "Petershams" in the world, the other two being in England and Australia. However, those two pronounce it "Peter-shum", whereas we say "Peter-SAM". Thus, it truly is a one-of-a-kind place. Throughout my life, whenever I told somebody I came from Petersham, that person would invariably ask, "Where's that?" The line we natives always used in response was, "It's in central Mass., but don't blink or you'll miss it." Then when I attended college in upstate New York, I quickly learned to just say, "Boston" when asked where I was from, because that's what everybody assumed anyway once they heard my accent. The irony in that answer is that Petersham is actually EIGHTY miles west of Boston, and 99% of Bostonians have never heard of, nor will ever step foot in Petersham.

At a very early age I learned that my town had two main claims to fame. The first happened in February of 1787, when General Benjamin Lincoln and his army surprised Daniel Shays and his men in Petersham, which resulted in the end of Shays' Rebellion. Prior to their defeat, Shays and his men had exposed the weakness of the new country's Articles of Confederation, thereby showing the need for a more centralized and powerful federal government. Shays' Rebellion played a key role in the passage of the United States Constitution later that year, thus cementing Petersham's place in this nation's history.

The second signature event in town took place in June of 1953, when one of the worst natural disasters ever to hit Massachusetts materialized. A tornado started in Petersham, then quickly tore through town after town before it finally died out some fifty miles east in Framingham. The Worcester Tornado, as it would come to be known, killed nearly 100 people and left another 10,000 homeless. It still ranks as one of the twenty deadliest tornadoes in the history of the United States, and it began in Petersham. In the 166 years between the end of Shays' Rebellion and the beginning of the Worcester Tornado, not much went on in 01366 that made the rest of the world take note. People worked their farms, they went to church, and they raised their families, and no-

viii

body outside the town lines paid them any mind. The locals long had a saying, "it's a quiet little town, and we kind of like it that way."

But, as with every other small New England town, Petersham does have its share of stories — some true, some apocryphal. It is said that Calvin Coolidge liked to visit with a good friend who had a house on Carter Pond, and there the two men would fish off the back porch while drinking Moxies. They would sit there fishing for hours on end without a word passing between them, which was just how "Silent Cal" liked it. Or so the story goes. Then there's the Legend of Rum Rock. One stormy night many years ago, a stagecoach carrying a full load of rum crashed over a rock formation off of Popple Camp Road, killing the driver and smashing his cargo all over the rocks. As a boy I was told that during a full moon one could still smell the rum coming off of those rocks all those years later! Finally, in my youth the town also claimed that the Petersham Country Store was the oldest continually run country store in the United States. This was a claim that no one anywhere in the rest of the country either knew or cared enough about to try and disprove, which we naturally took as validation of our claim. Oh, and then there's this — Bill Cosby once owned a house in town. When I was younger everyone had a story of seeing him here or there — my brother Bob actually did wait on him in the Country Store one time — but now we just pretend like none of that ever happened, for obvious reasons.

In any case, whenever local historians got to spinning those and other yarns about our little Hilltop Town, they would invariably touch on a tiny nugget that piqued my curiosity the very first time I heard it. As the story went, the last man ever to be hanged in Massachusetts came from Petersham. His last name was Frost, and he had murdered someone in town, for whatever reason. Having been convicted of the crime, he was then sentenced to death by hanging. At his execution, as the noose was placed around his neck, he was asked if he had any last words. With surprising aplomb he yelled out, "There will be a Frost in Hell tonight!" As soon as he uttered those words, the floor opened up and he plunged to his death.

When I first caught wind of that story, I remember thinking that Frost's final declaration was just about the coolest thing I'd ever heard. And as I listened to the tale in subsequent years, I found my-self mouthing those eight words right along with the storyteller. At one time I even tried to figure out where that ranked in the history of famous "last words." I surmised that it belonged somewhere between

Nathan Hale's "I only regret that I have but one life to lose for my country," and George Sanders' "I am leaving you because I'm bored," found in the actor's suicide note.

But while Frost's last words had made an indelible impression on me, they'd also left me with two nagging questions. One, who was the man who uttered that should-be-famous phrase? Surely a character with such panache deserves to be remembered as more than just a "man named Frost." After all, he uttered those words at a time in our history when men simply did not joke about "going to Hell," especially when death was imminent. Second, what specifically did this "man named Frost" do that led to a noose being placed around his neck? After all, there have been hundreds of thousands of capital crimes committed in the history of Massachusetts, but very few actually resulted in the death penalty. In fact, the official statistic is there have only been 345 such public executions, and the first 99 of those occurred in the 1600s. (Most of those were for the crimes of witchcraft or piracy.) So what made this man from my little town one of the very select few who were made to pay the ultimate price; what did he do *exactly*? At a base level this book sets out to provide the answers to those two nagging questions.

But there are two other reasons why I chose to write about this story. When I wrote my first book, *ACK in Ashes: Nantucket's Great Fire of 1846*, I did so in part as a way of challenging myself. In that case the challenge was: could I actually write a book? Having climbed that mountain, I decided that the challenge for my second such effort would be: could I actually tell an interesting story about something that happened in a place where seemingly nothing ever happened? I first kicked around the idea of *Fishin' With "Silent Cal,"* but that book would have been even more boring than, well, actually fishing with "Silent Cal." Not long after dismissing that idea, the thought occurred to me: who doesn't love a good murder story? With that thought, *A Frost In Hell* was born. And while it's true this book centers around a murder, it's about much more than that. This is the story of how people in a quiet little farming town dealt with something that was never supposed to happen in their quiet little farming town. How did those people, who had almost no experience in dealing with something like this, how did they step up to *that* challenge?

Then there's the second reason why I wanted to write this book. The one thing that has always semi-irritated me about Petersham's two claims to fame is: they aren't *really* "Petersham" stories. Yes, Shays'

Rebellion ended there, but neither Daniel Shays nor General Lincoln was from Petersham. And yes, the tornado in 1953 started in Petersham, but it has forever more been known as the *Worcester* Tornado, and Petersham was the least affected of all the towns that were ravaged by it. In fact, none of the 94 people killed by that tornado were in Petersham. Thus, while my town has a connection to both events, neither are "Petersham" at their core. This story is. Now, I'll grant you that it may sound a bit odd that I am seemingly speaking with pride about a murder. Allow me to stipulate the following: the murderer, that "man named Frost," he's not *really* a Petersham man. He only lived there for two years; he was a drifter more than anything else. But the people who solved the crime, the people who brought the murderer to justice, the people who carried on long after Frost was in Hell, *they* were Petersham men and women. That's where my pride comes in.

In the end, I wrote this book because I wanted to share a story with you about something that really happened in my town. I loved growing up in Petersham — putting on that Little League uniform on game days, running around the bandstand during band concerts, swimming in Brown's Pond with my buddies in the summer, sledding down the hill behind the Town Hall with my buddies in the winter, riding my bike to the old Center School when the snow had finally melted, wondering what crazy animal made that noise in the woods while playing flashlight tag, listening to a Red Sox game on the radio as I sat idly behind the counter at the Country Store, failing to muster up the courage to sweet-talk that really pretty girl who walked into the store that one day — you get the idea. A small town New England upbringing may not have been for everybody, but it was definitely for me, and I wouldn't change mine for the world. Except, if I could have maybe just one thing back, I might actually say something to that girl who walked into the store that day. Who knows, maybe I'd ask her if she wanted to go to a band concert with me, and maybe she'd say, "There will be a frost in Hell before that happens." And then I'd say, "Great, so I'll see you at six…"

Doug "VB" Goudie
vbthewise.com
@vbthewise
July 2018

Bubba Goudie

1982

PETERSHAM POST #415
Barre Little League
Petersham, Massachusetts

PRO CARD

COMMONWEALTH OF MASSACHUSETTS,
COUNTY OF WORCESTER,
WORCESTER, May 5, 1876.

Sir: In obedience to the laws of this commonwealth relating to the sentence of death, I hereby request your presence at the jail in Worcester, in said county, on Friday, the 26th day of May, current, punctually at ten o'clock in the forenoon, for the purpose of witnessing the execution of Samuel J. Frost, a convict, of the crime of murder. By signifying your acceptance of this request a card of admission will be furnished you.

A. B. R. SPRAGUE, Sheriff.

The official invitation to the Frost execution.
(As printed in *The Worcester Daily Spy* in May of 1876)

The Execution
May 26, 1876

As the 257 invited guests chatted nervously while staring at the clock on the north wall of the Guard Room inside the jail on Summer Street, Worcester County Sheriff Augustus B.R. Sprague studied the second hand of his pocket watch. When it finally reached the "12" at the top, making the time exactly 10:30am, Sheriff Sprague closed the watch, cleared his throat, and then said to the assembled spectators, "Gentlemen, I have to respectfully request that you will remain as quiet as possible during the time you are in the Guard Room." As soon as he spoke those words two things happened: the small talk ceased immediately, and the tension in the room rose precipitously. It was "go time", and for only the third instance in the last fifty years Worcester County in Massachusetts was about to publicly execute someone.

Sheriff Sprague exited the Guard Room following his instruction, and as the door closed behind him the nervous anticipation of 256 of the 257 spectators was palpable. The crowd consisted of seemingly every law enforcement official in Worcester County, as well as the sheriffs from Hampshire County, Franklin County, and even Windham County in Vermont. Every newspaper in the state had at least one reporter in the room, and the first several rows of spectators were filled almost exclusively with journalists. Sprague had issued different colored admission cards for witnesses, reporters, and general spectators, and those cards had given preferred seating to the first two groups. Many local officials and prominent businessmen were also in attendance that morning to satiate their macabre curiosity. In fact, the demand for tickets to the execution had been at least five times the number made available by Sheriff Sprague, and the streets outside the jail were lined with people who desperately wanted to be inside. This was undeniably a once-in-a-lifetime event (literally for one man) that these witnesses would be able to brag about having attended, so those that were in the room felt very fortunate to be there. Everyone that is, except for one man.

The husband of the condemned man's sister sat quietly alone in the Guard Room, full of dread for what was about to happen. He was there to witness the event on behalf of his wife's family, and he had been tasked with bringing his doomed brother-in-law's body back home to New Hampshire after it was over. For him, the day had already been surreal. Just an hour earlier he had been in a prison cell talking with his brother-in-law, who was surprisingly upbeat and seemingly unfazed by what the law had in store for him. Now he was mere minutes away from watching that same man die. He had tried to prepare himself for what was about to happen, but now that the moment had arrived it was much harder than he had anticipated. Little did he know, it was about to get drastically worse.

As quickly as the door to the Guard Room had closed, it now re-opened, and the death march began. Sheriff Sprague entered first, followed by his Deputy David Earle of Worcester, who was all but invisible to the crowd because of who walked in beside him — the man of the hour, the person everyone had come to see — Samuel J. Frost. For most of the spectators in the room it was their first glimpse of the evildoer they had read so much about, and what caught them all by surprise was just how small he was. Most reporters guessed him to be 5'5", and they put his weight at no more than 120 pounds. His small frame bewildered the crowd because for months the newspapers had portrayed Frost as a larger than life monster, but now they were seeing that he was just a little rat of a man, even by 1876 standards. For the occasion he was dressed almost entirely in black: black trousers, a black shirt with matching black vest, all layered under a black frock coat. The only clothing on him that wasn't black was the seemingly unnecessary pair of light brown gloves over his hands, which had been crossed in front of his chest and then strapped down. And while the crowd was tense as Frost entered the room, he apparently wasn't. One newspaper noted, "his step was firm and elastic, and he carelessly glanced around" as he walked in, and he did not need to brace himself on Deputy Earle in any way. In other words, if he was trying to give the appearance of being apathetic about what was soon to happen to him, he was doing a good job of it.

Following immediately behind Frost into the Guard Room was the Reverend C.M. Lamson, the minister who had attempted to be the condemned man's spiritual advisor. Lamson's Congregational Church on Salem Street was less than a mile from the jail on Summer Street, which enabled the clergyman to visit Frost quite frequently in the last few weeks. Unfortunately for Lamson, Frost would have none of the reverend's religious talk, and so the two spent most of their time together playing checkers and discussing politics. Behind Lamson walked Deputy A.W. Keene from the nearby town of Milford, and bringing up the rear of the procession was Deputy Sylvester Bothwell of Barre, the man who had initially arrested Frost just ten months earlier.

The men walked around nearly three-quarters of the scaffold in order to get to the stairs, and as they approached those stairs all eyes were of course on Frost. In the weeks leading up to this day, Frost had told anyone who cared to listen that he would have no trouble walking right up to the noose that awaited him – his exact words were that he "intended to die game". However, most people dismissed his statement as false bravado from a secretly scared man. But just as he had when he entered the Guard Room, Frost remained steadfast and deliberate in his movements, and he effortlessly climbed the twelve steps leading up to the platform. In fact, one reporter for *The Fitchburg Sentinel* noted that when Frost "reached the last step of the stairs he swayed a little, enough to show that he was making a desperate effort to appear unconcerned." (By contrast, Thomas Piper, who was hanged that very same morning in Boston for multiple murders, stumbled and needed help on his way up to the gallows, and he cried loudly once he got there.) Upon reaching the ten by twelve foot platform perched some ten feet above the Guard Room floor, Frost stepped to the center where a chair had been placed next to "the drop" just for him. As he sat down, Deputy Earle took his position behind Frost, while Deputies Keene and Bothwell assumed positions on either side of him.

Once Frost was seated, Reverend Lamson stepped forward and offered the following prayer:

> Our Father God, in this terrible moment we confess thy power, thy wisdom, and thy mercy. Thou art our creator. Thou didst give this man the life which he is about to surrender. Bless thee the state which for the sake of safety and purity is about to perform this awful, this solemn act. Oh God have mercy upon this man, receive thou his soul to thyself. Meet him now, and conduct him thyself to thyself, and in thy presence may he have mercy for the sake of Jesus Christ our Lord and Savior. Amen and amen.

Lamson then stepped to the side of the platform and silently waited for the death of the man he had come to know well over the last several weeks. (During the most recent execution in the Worcester Jail, that of the James brothers in 1868, the presiding chaplain that day, the Reverend R.R. Shippen, delivered the prayer but did not stay to witness the executions.)

At this point in the proceedings, the condemned man sometimes would be asked if he had any last words, but Sheriff Sprague had told Frost the night before that this was not going to happen. Because this was only the third public execution to take place in Worcester County in the last fifty years, and more importantly because it was the first under Sheriff Sprague's watch, he wanted no shenanigans during the proceedings. Sprague feared that Frost might ramble on for some time if given the chance, and so even though Frost had expressed a desire to speak from the gallows, Sprague had turned him down. Instead, he afforded Frost the opportunity to write a final statement the night before, and Sprague promised to give that statement to the press after the execution had been carried out (which he did). And so as Frost sat in silence, it was Sprague's voice that followed Lamson's. He began the verbatim reading of Frost's death warrant, which had been issued by Secretary of State Henry B. Pierce on behalf of Governor Alexander Rice of the Commonwealth of Massachusetts:

> Whereas at a term of our Supreme Judicial Court, begun and holden at Worcester, within and for the County of Worcester, on the first Tuesday of October, being the fifth day of said month, in the year of our Lord one thousand eight hundred and seventy-five, Samuel J. Frost of Petersham, in said county, was convicted of the crime of Murder in the First Degree, and thereupon, by our said Court, the said Samuel J. Frost was sentenced, for said crime, to suffer the pains of Death by being hanged "by the neck till he be dead;" all of which, by an Exemplification of the Record of said Court, which we have caused to be hereunto annexed, doth to us fully appear.

When Sheriff Sprague mentioned Frost's name in the warrant, Deputy Earle placed his hands under Frost's arms indicating that it was time for Frost to stand up, which he did. Deputy Keene then moved the chair away while Deputy Earle commenced tying Frost's legs together, both at the knees and ankles. Earle then positioned Frost exactly in the center of "the drop", and as he did so, Keene removed the two pins that prevented "the drop" from being activated by the foot trigger located at Sprague's feet. Deputy Earle next removed a black hood from his jacket pocket and placed it over Frost's head. Finally, Earle took hold of the noose that had been dangling above the men, placed it around Frost's neck and cinched it firmly. (The newspapers had noted the day before the execution that the rope to be used had been made of "the finest imported Italian hemp"!) Frost now had mere seconds to live, but true to his word, he never did give any indication of dread or fear even as they tied him up and put the hood on him. As the deputies prepared Frost to be hanged, Sheriff Sprague continued his monotone reading of the warrant:

> We therefore command you, that upon Friday, the twenty-sixth day of May, in the year eighteen hundred and seventy-six, between the hours of nine o'clock before noon and twelve o'clock, meridian, of the same day; within the walls of the prison of said county, or within the enclosed yard of such prison, in said county of Worcester, agreeably to the provisions of the one hundred and seventy fourth chapter of Our General Statutes, you cause execution of said sentence of our said Court, in all respects to be done and performed upon him, the said Samuel J. Frost, for which this shall be your sufficient warrant.
> Whereof fail not at your peril, and make Return of this Warrant with your doings thereof into our Secretary's office, as soon as may be after you shall have executed the same.

Upon reading those last few words, Sheriff Sprague folded the warrant in his hands, gave a quick glance back to ensure that Frost was in place, and then announced matter-of-factly, "I now proceed to execution." Before anybody in the crowd had time to brace for what was about to happen, Sprague jammed his foot on the trigger of "the drop," sending Frost and the noose down through the square hole in the scaffold. It had taken just eight minutes from the time Sprague had closed his pocket watch until he stepped on that trigger, and things had gone exactly as he and his men had planned.

While all eyes in the room were watching Frost's body fall, Sprague's ears were hard at work too, because at that very moment he wanted to make sure he DIDN'T hear something. During the early planning stages for Frost's execution, Sprague had talked to several witnesses of the James brothers' executions in 1868. Those witnesses had all mentioned to Sprague that there was an awful noise made by "the drop" when it banged against the bottom of the platform after the trigger had been pressed. The noise was jarring and distracting they'd said, and so Sprague had asked William Sibley, the man tasked with building the scaffold, if he could install a rubber stopper on the underside of "the drop" to muffle any sound as "the drop" hit the bottom of the platform. Sure enough, as Sprague stood there with his foot still on the trigger, he heard not a sound from "the drop." In that moment, Sprague was completely satisfied that the execution had gone off without a hitch.

And then all hell broke loose.

Although there had been no sound of "the drop" clanging in the Guard Room that morning, there was a noise heard as Frost fell the seven and a half feet towards the floor — a loud collective gasp from the spectators. They had seen something that Sprague could not from his vantage point, and it had horrified each and every one of them. In fact, the sight was so gruesome that it would transform what otherwise might have been a page 3 or 4 news item into a nationwide page 1 story. It would also cement Samuel J. Frost's place in the history of Massachusetts' jurisprudence.

The *New York Times'* headline the next day read "Death By the Hangman: A Horrible Scene at the Scaffold." *The Minneapolis Tribune's* headline was "Execution: One of the Most Horrible Scenes Ever Recorded." *The Philadelphia Inquirer* went with the alliterative "Shocking Scene on a Scaffold." *The Nebraska State Journal* described it as "A Sickening Scene at the Execution." *The National Republican* in Washington D.C. exclaimed "The Petersham Murderer: A Frightful and Bloody Scene on the Gallows." And the local newspaper, *The Fitchburg Daily Sentinel*, screamed in big block letters "A GHASTLY SPECTACLE!"

What happened? Well, the best description of the horror was found in *The Baltimore Sun* of May 27th, 1876, under the unsensational headline "Execution of the Petersham Murderer." It read as follows:

> When the body fell at the scaffold the first thrill of a shudder had not run through the spectators when the body was seen spinning at the end of the rope almost headless, a fearful tear extending over the front of the throat and the blood gushing out in streams. The blood, forced upward by the arterial move-

ments, spurted fountainlike upward from one to two feet, the
stream falling to the floor in a circle round the hanging body.
This circle extended even to the framework of the gallows,
which was in many places sprinkled with blood. The blood
poured from the wound down the front of the body and trickled from the feet, forming a pool directly beneath the body. For
some two minutes the arterial gurglings of blood continued.
The knot of the rope had been placed behind Frost's left ear
almost around the centre of the neck. The drop was enough not
only to break his neck but to sever the spinal column entirely,
leaving the body hanging by the integuments of the rear portion
only.

How grotesque the scene must have been to the spectators
"lucky" enough to witness the "arterial gurglings of blood" continuing
on for two whole minutes as Frost's lifeless body spun slowly around
and around. (Remember, this was 100 years before Hollywood special effects would make such a scene only slightly less shocking.) In
fact, one month after *The Baltimore Sun* published its version of Frost's
execution, *The Abbeville Press* in South Carolina reprinted the *Sun's*
account on page 1 of its June 28th, 1876 edition. The only difference
was that at the end of its reprinting, *The Abbeville Press* added the line
"This recital doubtless seems full of horrors, but it falls far short of the
realities of the scene." Of that there could be little doubt.

After that initial collective gasp from the crowd, the Guard
Room again fell silent, except for the spinning rope and the dripping
blood. Everyone in the room was frozen, not knowing how to process
what they were seeing. And that included the sheriff who had tried to
think of everything, right down to the last detail of the rubber stopper.
As *The Worcester West Chronicle* put it the next day:

> None felt keener the ghastly sight presented, than Sheriff
> Sprague; for minutes he seemed horror stricken and speechless,
> but with a consciousness that he had taken every precaution
> against accident, and performed his whole duty faithfully, he
> soon revived, and requested that all but the physicians to with-
> draw from the room.

The spectators didn't need to be told twice; as soon as Sprague asked
everyone to clear the room they scurried out, desperate to find some

air and maybe a way to erase the last twenty minutes from their minds. In very short order the only men left in the Guard Room were Sprague, his deputies, a few reporters, and a multitude of physicians, three of whom had been assigned the task of determining whether or not Frost was actually dead. Obviously he was; his head had been almost completely severed, and his body had spurted out most of its blood. But the formality of an official confirmation of death required that these three men go through the motions. Thus, one by one Doctor Rufus Woodward of Worcester, Dr. G.A. Bates of Worcester, and Doctor George Jewett of Fitchburg each checked Frost's bloodied torso for a heartbeat. Finding none, each man in turn nodded in Sprague's direction to indicate that the death warrant had indeed been faithfully carried out.

Sprague then ordered Frost's body to be cut down and placed on a stretcher for a prearranged immediate autopsy. The autopsy had not been set up at the behest of Frost's family (they knew well in advance what the cause of death was going to be), but rather it had been requested by the medical community as a means of studying the effects and ramifications of death by hanging. In fact, there were SEVEN doctors who had agreed to take part in examining Frost's remains, all in the interest of science. *The Worcester Daily Spy* noted their findings the next day:

> When the body was examined it was found that the spinal column was broken between the second and third vertebrae. The ligaments and arteries were all broke, except the large one at the back of the neck, which alone held the body and head together. The parting of the flesh is accounted for by the fact that Frost was always a hard working man, and having been confined with comparatively little exercise for ten months, his flesh had become soft, and offered little or no resistance to the rope cutting through. Upon the removal of the cap it was found that the eyes had not been closed, and in points attending death by hanging, Dr. L. S. Dixon examined them, and found that the capsule of the lens of the eye was not ruptured, which is claimed to be a remarkable fact.

Once Dixon and his colleagues had completed their work, Frost's body was placed in a coffin, and Sprague immediately signed it over to Frost's shell-shocked brother-in-law, who was somehow able to function in spite of what he had just witnessed. At that point both he and Sheriff

Sprague just wanted to bring the whole nightmarish episode to an end. The brother-in-law did just that by hightailing it to the nearest train station, where he boarded the 3:25pm for Boston with the coffin of Samuel J. Frost in tow.

Sheriff Sprague wouldn't get away so easily however, as he still had work to do. He and his deputies now had to clean up the pools of blood congealing on the floor of the Guard Room. And as they did so, the dumbfounded sheriff kept replaying the morning's events over in his head, and he kept thinking that everything had gone so well initially. But in an instant, at precisely 10:38am, it had all suddenly gone to hell. Just like Samuel J. Frost.

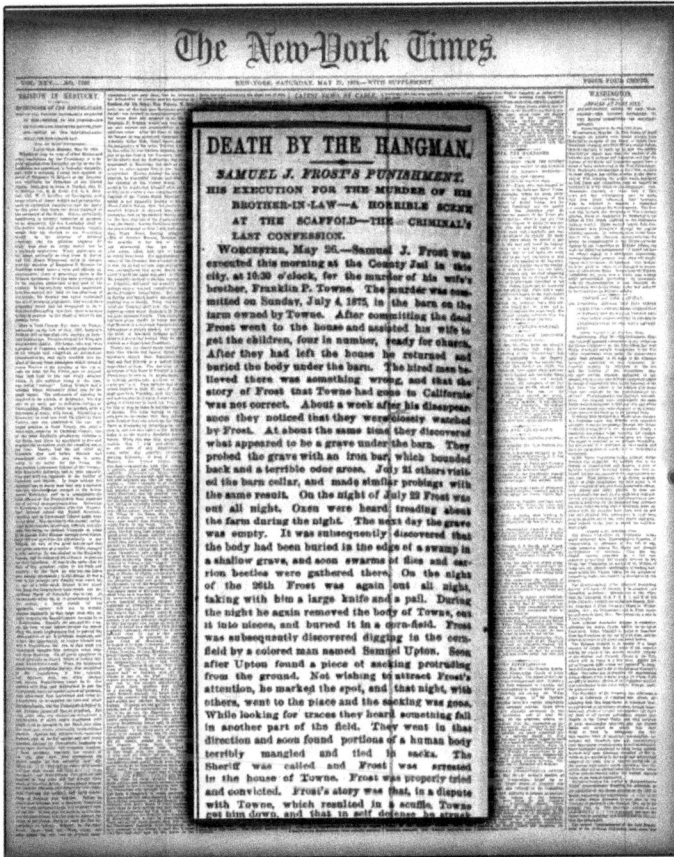

The New York Times on May 26, 1876.
(Courtesy of newspapers.com)

The only known photo of the Frost house.
(Photo courtesy of the Petersham Historical Society)

2

<u>The Murder</u>

Franklin Pingree Towne awoke a little before 5:00am on the morning of July 4th, 1875. While most people throughout the nation were waking up to celebrate the 99th anniversary of the country's birth, Frank Towne was rising to go meet his death. He didn't know it of course, but someone else in that house did — his brother-in-law Samuel Joseph Frost. Frost and his wife Carrie had purchased the farmhouse on the corner of Hardwick and Dana roads in Petersham in January of 1873, and they had let Frank (Carrie's brother) live there off and on ever since. In fact, Towne was currently in the middle of a one-year lease of the farm on the property from his brother-in-law, which is why he was up early on that holiday morning — he had farming chores to tend to. Towne sleepily put on the same shirt he wore every day to do his chores, a blue flannel shirt with the sleeves rolled up. (He actually had two of the same shirt, so it appeared as if he was always wearing THAT shirt.) Next, he put his gangly legs through his brown overalls and then pulled them up over his six-foot frame. He passed his hands through his hair a few times, rubbed the scraggly beard on his face, and after a deep exhale, he was ready to start another long day of farming. His first task was to be milking his cows.

Frank crept quietly down the stairs from his bedroom on the left side of the second floor, walking as gingerly as he could in his stocking feet. The staircase led right into the south bedroom on the first floor of the house, where three of his sister's children were sleeping, and he didn't want to wake them. He proceeded through the open door of the south bedroom into the kitchen, where he paused only long enough to pick up his three milking pails (two twelve-quart pails and an eight-quart pail). Continuing through the kitchen towards the front entryway, he passed the north bedroom on his right where his brother-in-law Samuel was sleeping, along with the Frosts' youngest child, Annie, who had just turned two the day before. When he reached the doorway at the front of the house, Frank jammed his feet into his boots that he always left there overnight, he grabbed his felt hat hanging just to the right of the door, and he headed outside towards the barn where his three cows were waiting. His day was just starting; his life would soon be ending.

Not long after Frank left the house, Samuel J. Frost rose from his bed, got dressed, and then he too walked out the kitchen door and headed towards the barn. But unlike Frank, when Samuel got to the entryway of the barn he didn't step in straight away. Instead, he paused to look inside the barn, where he saw Frank milking the red heifer with his back to the door. (Frank's three cows were known as the "red heifer", the "white-faced heifer", and the "starred heifer".) As he surveyed the scene inside, Samuel knew it was now or never if he was going to do the dastardly deed he'd been thinking about for some time. This was likely the last chance he would have to be alone with Frank for the foreseeable future, as the farmhands who had gone away for the holiday weekend were set to return soon. In fact, George Josselyn, who worked for Frank, was supposed to return to the farm at some point that afternoon. Additionally, Frank had told Samuel that he was planning on attending church that morning, and so he'd be leaving the farm around 10:00am. That meant that there was a chance Frank might not be back before Josselyn's arrival. (Josselyn would return at 4:00pm as it turned out.) Time was running out for Frost; he was staring at his last real chance, and he knew it.

Frost had a golden opportunity the day before to do what he had in mind, but he had chickened out. After both men had finished their daily chores that Saturday, Frost had asked Towne if he wanted to go swimming. When Towne said "yes", the two men took Frost's horse across several meadows behind the farm to a river located there. The men were alone for some time in a very remote area some two miles south of their property, and Frost must have considered taking out his brother-in-law then. But he had a two-fold problem then: one, he wasn't quite sure how to go about doing it, and two, Frank was much larger than he — Towne was 6 feet tall and weighed 165 pounds, Frost was at least half a foot shorter and weighed 125. Had it been Towne looking to take out Frost, he could have drowned him there in the river, but that was not a realistic option for the smaller Frost. So he had abandoned the idea then, and the two men simply swam together for a while and then went home. When they got back to the farm that evening, Towne headed into town for some more frivolity while Frost stayed back and went to bed early. As he lay awake in bed that night, he played dozens of scenarios over in his head, but he never could settle on how best to do what he had in mind. He was frustrated; he knew what he must do, but he couldn't figure out how. His anxiety was growing by the minute, and his chances were fading by the second. It had been a restless Saturday night for Frost, to say the least.

So as he stood there that Sunday morning glaring at his brother-in-law, he knew there was no turning back. As he stared inside the barn, he suddenly spotted a broken off piece of iron from an old sledgehammer on the floor of the barn. Samuel had borrowed that sledge from his neighbor Norman Loring for the expressed purpose of pounding some knobs onto the horns of his steers back in January, which he had done with the help of an Irishman named Mike Glennon. But a few weeks later, while the two men dug out a drain in the cellar of Frost's house, Irish Mike had broken the sledge right down the middle, and one half of the iron head had splintered off the handle. It was that very same jagged chunk of iron that was now staring back at Frost as he was pondering what he was going to do, when suddenly it all became clear. He stepped up into the barn (the opening was a foot or so above the ground), picked up the iron and crept up behind Frank, who was sitting on a stool milking the red heifer. Without hesitating, Frost drove the broken piece of iron as hard as he could into the right side of Towne's head, right behind his ear. Towne let out a stunned but muted "by gorry!" upon being hit (that was the 1875 equivalent of 'OMG!', originating from the Irish term 'begorrah'). Before Towne could react, Frost jumped on him, and raising both hands above his head, he drove the iron piece down into Towne's face, crushing his nose. He pulled the weapon up once more as Towne collapsed and slammed it down again, this time crashing it into Towne's mouth, shattering three of his front teeth. Frost then stood up, his heart racing while he gripped the iron piece even tighter in case he might still need it. Blood oozed out of Towne's broken mouth and from behind his ear, but otherwise he lay still. The first blow had crushed the lower part of Towne's skull, while the second and third blows had smashed in his face. The attack had lasted no more than thirty seconds, but Frost had finally done what he had long set out to do. He had killed his brother-in-law.

Samuel stood over the body for several minutes, both to insure that Frank was indeed dead, and because he didn't know what else to do. When he finally stepped back, he inadvertently kicked over the eight-quart pail Frank had been using for his milking. Frost quickly moved the red heifer into another stall, and then he rolled Towne's body up against the side of the barn in the stall where it lay. He located an old sheet of wood and leaned it against the wall, concealing Towne's corpse. It wasn't perfect, but no one was expected to be in that barn for a while, so the temporary lean-to would do in the short term. Frost exhaled for a minute, and then he inexplicably picked up Towne's now empty milk pail and carried it over to the doorway of the barn, where he sat down to try and gather himself. He perched in the entryway stoically for several minutes, thinking not only about what he had just done, but also about what he was still going to have to do. Having temporarily shielded the body from view, he decided his next priority was to act as if nothing had happened. That was going to be so easy however, as he would soon learn.

He hoisted himself up from the entryway, grabbed the pail, and headed back into the house. He set the empty bucket down on the kitchen counter (that would turn out to be a big mistake, as you'll see) and asked his wife Carrie about breakfast. She told him it wasn't quite ready, so Frost went into the parlor off the kitchen and sat down to read the Bible. (Frost was definitively NOT a God-fearing man, so his thumbing through the Bible would seem suspicious to anyone paying attention.) He opened to the fifth chapter of Job and read, "For wrath killeth the foolish man, and envy slayeth the silly one." But while his eyes were going over the words, his mind was somewhere else. He was still thinking about what lay in the barn and how he was ultimately going to dispose of his brother-in-law's body. Frost stared blankly at the Bible page half-reading, when suddenly his four-year-old daughter Emma walked in and snapped Frost out of his trance. "Breakfast is ready," she said with her soft voice, and she then wandered back into the kitchen. Frost closed the Bible and followed little Emma to the breakfast table. (Lest the Bible anecdote read like a bad Hollywood script, it was none other than Frost himself who would testify during his trial about having read Job chapter 5 that morning.)

While the next few hours were certainly going to be hectic for Samuel J. Frost, it is worth noting what had just happened in the last two hours of his life. He awoke in bed next to his two-year-old daughter Annie; an hour and a half later he was told, "breakfast is ready" by his four-year-old daughter Emma. In between those two angelic moments, Frost had premeditatedly bludgeoned his girls' "Uncle Frank" to death with a broken piece of sledgehammer.

Frost sat down to breakfast with his two girls (and his two boys) but as he would later testify, "I don't think I ate a great deal." He didn't say too much either, but that wasn't overly unusual for him. Following breakfast, Frost sat down on the steps of the front door off the kitchen. It was then that his wife Carrie asked him the million-dollar question: "Where's Frank?" Her brother usually joined them for breakfast, and she had expected him to do so that morning, but Carrie spoke the words more in puzzlement than in accusation. Samuel was ready for the question however, and without flinching he gave his answer. He and Frank had scuffled that morning in the barn, he said, and he had blackened Frank's eye. Frank was so embarrassed about what happened that he had stormed off to the pasture behind the barn to cool down. It seemed odd to Carrie that Samuel hadn't mentioned the fight until then, but she had no real reason to be overly suspicious at that point. Thus, as was often the case with their small talk, she let her husband's story go unchecked rather than press the matter. Samuel then stood up and told Carrie she should start getting ready for church, and he nonchalantly volunteered to help get their boys ready (seven-year-old Charles and six-year-old George) once he'd hitched his horse to the wagon for her. Carrie found Samuel's offer a tad strange considering that since they'd moved to Petersham, she could not remember a time when he had ever helped get the boys ready for church. But again, she wasn't in the habit of sassing her husband, so she said nothing. The service that day was some five miles away at the Congregational Church, and Carrie usually left the house a little after 10:00am to make church on time. But with Samuel's help, she and the boys were able to leave fifteen minutes earlier that Sunday morning. It was time Samuel could surely use.

As soon as the wagon started up the road, Frost stepped back inside the house to fetch his daughters. He then brought them outside, in the opposite direction of the barn, and he gave four-year-old Emma a doll and ordered her to stay there with her sister Annie and the family's dog. He then walked straight to the barn and got down to business. First, Frost secured a pick and shovel and went underneath the barn floor to the basement where he started digging. In just a short time he had dug a rectangular hole, approximately six feet long, two feet wide, and close to two feet deep. With that done he went back up into the barn to fetch his brother-in-law's body. Frost tried lifting Frank's corpse to carry it below, but he quickly realized the 165-pounds of dead weight were going to be too much for him to handle without help. Looking around, he spotted a pair of leather horse straps hanging on the wall across the barn. He looped them around Towne's arms, then pulled the straps over his shoulders, leaned forward and pulled.

The straps worked, and by using all his strength he was able to drag the body to a side door which opened out over an embankment held up by a stone wall. He lowered the body onto the bank wall and then stepped around and under it, which allowed him to get his shoulders underneath the lifeless mass. Then, with more than a fair amount of difficulty, he carried the corpse across his back into the basement of the barn. He dropped his right shoulder enough to allow the body to slide off, causing it to fall into his makeshift grave with a thud. Next, he searched the barn for something with which to cover the body. Finding an old horse blanket, he laid it over his best friend and then shoveled all the recently removed dirt back into the hole. He patted it down as best he could, and as he wiped his forehead he stood looking down at his work. Although it wasn't perfect, he was pretty pleased to have that laborious chore finished.

He'd made good progress, but Frost was concerned about just how long Towne's burial had taken, so he returned to the house for a time check. It was only 11:00am; it hadn't taken him nearly as long as he feared. He still had at least an hour before his wife would be returning from church. So Samuel went back to the barn to see what else needed to be done. When he surveyed the interior of the barn, he noticed three things on the floor: the murder weapon, a watch, and a jackknife. The latter two items belonged to Towne and had fallen out of his pockets when Frost had dragged his body out. He put the watch and knife into his pants pocket, and then tried to figure out what to do with the murder weapon. After some thought, he picked up the blood-soaked iron piece and exited through the same barn door from which he had first seen the piece earlier that morning. After making sure there were no witnesses about, he threw the chunk of iron as far as he could across the street, and he watched it clear a stone wall located there. Satisfied, he re-entered the barn one last time to shovel some manure over the bloody floorboards where he had killed Towne.

With that completed, Frost was finished dealing with the immediate physical evidence of the crime, at least for the time being. It hadn't all gone smoothly, but Samuel was content in that moment. As he stepped outside the barn for the last time that morning, he also felt relieved knowing that he'd finally killed his brother-in-law. The thought had been weighing heavily upon him for some time; now at least it was done. And he still had some time to figure out what the next part of his story was going to be in regards to Frank's disappearance.

Carrie and the boys returned from church around 1:00 pm, and it wasn't long before she asked her husband if he'd seen Frank yet. Samuel said he had, and he told her "exactly" what happened. Frank had come back to the house a short time after Carrie had left, but he did so only to inform Samuel that he had decided to leave the farm and head to California. (It was plausible enough, or so Samuel thought, because Frank had siblings living in California with whom Frank had stayed for several months a few years prior. Also, it was not out of character for Frank to travel on short notice; he had done so several times in the decade Samuel had known him.) Further, Frank was so incensed about the altercation that morning that he had decided to go to Worcester immediately, on foot no less (Worcester was some thirty miles southeast of Petersham), so as to make train arrangements for his westward travel. Carrie asked why Frank would leave without first saying goodbye to her. Samuel suggested that Frank was far too angry to sit around waiting for Carrie to get back. In fact, Frost claimed that he had begged Frank not to leave without at least first settling their business affairs, but Frank wouldn't hear of it. Instead, Frank barked back that if Samuel still cared that much about it in a couple of days, then Samuel should go to Worcester on Wednesday and the two could settle up then before Towne left for good. Samuel said he'd agreed to that plan, and it was his hope that he might be able to convince Frank to return to the farm when he met up with him then. Samuel even surmised that a couple of days away could do Frank some good, as it might help him clear his head a little. In any case, that was how Frank had left it, according to Samuel.

The story made little sense to Carrie, but there wasn't much she could do about it at that moment. After all, she had no idea what had really transpired between the two men. She sensed something was up, and she knew that "J" (her pet name for her husband) was acting strangely, but to what end? She wasn't about to call her husband a liar (wives simply did not do that back in 1875), so at that point her only real option was to let things play out until Samuel went to Worcester on Wednesday. She'd rightly sensed that Samuel was being deceptive, but she wasn't yet considering the idea that her husband had just murdered her brother. However, it wouldn't be long before she'd come around to that idea, and once that happened, Carrie Frost would have a decision to make.

Selectman Alfred Peckham
(Photo courtesy of the Petersham Historical Society)

3

<u>The Cover-Up</u>

At first blush, all seemed "normal" on the Frost farm in the days following Frank Towne's disappearance. George Josselyn (Towne's employee) came back late in the afternoon of the 4th, and John Rathbone (Frost's help) returned in the early morning hours of the 5th. John brought his brother Charles with him, as Charles had agreed to work the farm that Monday in exchange for John's having had the previous Friday off. Upon their returns, the three men inquired of Towne, and Frost told them of his "scuffle" with Frank and Frank's subsequent "plan" to go to California. All three men doubted the story as soon as they'd heard it, since Towne had never once mentioned California to any of them before they'd left for the holiday. Like Carrie however, they didn't yet know what the real story was, and so they too decided to see what came of Samuel's Worcester visit. Plus, the chores on the farm had backed up over the long weekend, so their was plenty of hard work to be done which kept them from focusing too much on the missing Frank mystery.

As for Frost, he too had his hands full. With Towne "missing", Samuel now had to take full control of both the farm and the help. His first move was to ask Josselyn if he would stay on while they waited to see if Towne might return, which George agreed to do. (When his friend and boss didn't materialize by Wednesday night however, Josselyn left the farm for good that Thursday morning.) Frost also asked Charles Rathbone to stay on, and after fulfilling previous commitments elsewhere, he returned on the 11th and moved into the Frost house with his brother. (Charles was nine years older than John, his decision to return was surely based in part on a desire to protect his little brother.) But while Frost desperately needed the Rathbones' help on the farm, he quickly grew concerned about them. The Rathbone boys would later testify that the moment they'd returned to the farm, they felt like Frost was constantly watching and checking on them, something he had not been doing prior to the 4th. (If Samuel had wanted to "act natural", he was apparently failing.) And Frost had reason to be concerned.

     Aside from all the farming work he now had on his plate, Frost also had that dead body to deal with! While his initial 'Towne-to-California' story had bought him some time, it hadn't bought him *that* much time. Samuel's number one priority was making sure he got away with Frank's murder, but now the farm was crawling with people, unlike the morning of the 4th. Suspicion would surely be lurking, but it would remain just that as long as he could keep Towne's body concealed. If he could do that *and* keep his narrative consistent, he had a shot at pulling this off. To those ends, Frost decided upon three courses of action. As is so often the case in true crime stories however, his cover-up would prove to be even more self-destructive than his actual crime, and it would forever cement Samuel J. Frost's place in Massachusetts' criminal history.

Step 1 - The Worcester Story

     Frost had told his wife that Frank left the farm in a huff on Sunday morning and set out for Worcester, where Samuel was to meet him on Wednesday the 7th. As a result, Frost arose around 4:00am that morning, and as dawn quietly approached he mounted his sorrel horse and started off for Worcester. He would not make it back to the farm until well after dusk that evening, and unsurprisingly he did not have Towne with him when he returned. He did however have a brand new tale to tell when Carrie and the farmhands asked him what had happened:

> When I got to Worcester, I met Frank on Front Street at one of the saloons there. (Frost had worked for the C.C. Houghton Shoe and Boot Company on Front Street back in 1873.) I told Frank that I thought we could maybe work out our differences and he could come back here with me, but Frank immediately told me 'no'. He said he had made up his mind about California, and he wanted to settle up our business right then and there. I knew there was no point in arguing with him, so I said 'well, what should we do about the farm?' Frank said 'you need to buy me out.' We went back and forth a little on the price of that, but Frank finally said he'd take $300 for everything. I asked him if that included all his livestock, and he said he didn't have no use for them anymore anyways. I told him I didn't have $300 on me, and he said to give him what I had and then give him a note for the rest, so I gave him $125 in cash, and we wrote

up a note for the remainder of it. He was pretty happy to see that much cash, and he asked me how I had come by it. I told him I borrowed it from some friends I saw on my way in to see him, which is when I got this here. (Samuel had brought back a stone jar from his trip that he had lent a friend in Worcester a few months earlier.) I don't think Frank was expecting to get that money from me right then, so he got in a much better mood after I gave it to him. We finished our drinks, and Frank said he wanted to get a new pair of shoes for his trip, so we left the saloon and walked down to my old shop and got him some shoes. He gave me those over there at that time (Samuel nodded in the direction of Frank's old farming boots) 'cause he said he wouldn't be needing them no more. And that was it. Frank said he had to get going because his train was leaving at 5:00 and he wanted to say 'bye' to some people. I told him to let us know when he got himself settled out there in California, and I told him if things didn't work out he could always come back. He told me he'd see us all again sometime, and he told me to say 'bye' to you Carrie. And that was the last we said to each other. He was in pretty good spirits when I left him, and I know I couldn't have talked him out of it even if I tried. So that's what happened.

Frost felt pretty good about his story when he had finished telling it, but his audience didn't share his enthusiasm for it. For starters, Carrie couldn't imagine who amongst their friends could have lent Samuel $125 on such short notice. George Josselyn had never heard Frank talk about money in the way Frost described he had in that saloon. John Rathbone wondered why Towne would give Frost his old boots, and why would Frost take them, considering they were way too big for any of them to use. And all three wondered how it was that Samuel was able to find Frank so easily, considering the two men had made no such Front Street plans when Frank had left so abruptly on the 4th.

But this was still not the time to shout "liar!" While their doubts had now grown into full-blown suspicion, no one had any real proof that Samuel was lying and they still didn't know what the *real story* was. And they still had a little hope that Frank was alive somewhere, and that a much more plausible explanation for his absence would be coming. But those hopes had diminished with Samuel's latest story, and each of them had to now consider the possibility that Samuel had done something really bad to Frank. And yet that thought made very little sense to them also. After all, Samuel's having hurt or killed his best friend was just as unfathomable as Frank's having suddenly taken off to California, yet those were the two scenarios they were left to ponder at that time.

As an aside, while there is no disputing that the two men did *not* meet in Worcester that day (one of them was dead, after all), some questioned after the fact whether Frost ever actually went to the city on the 7th. Frost's proof that he had was that stone jar he had brought back from his "journey", but people were still skeptical. So much so in fact, that *The Worcester Daily Spy* did some asking around after Frost's arrest. They reported however in the August 4th edition that:

> several witnesses saw him at the grocery store of N.W. Holden on Front Street, where he called and wished to sell a small quantity of butter. Mr. Holden did not purchase of him, as he was already supplied.

But that tidbit didn't convince everyone. In fact, the day after *The Spy's* item ran, *The Worcester West Chronicle* had this story:

> The Wednesday after, Frost started (so he said) for Worcester, making a remarkably quick trip, and getting back about five that evening. Despite the run to Worcester, the horse did not seem fatigued.

Neither the horse's fatigue nor the failed butter sale ever came up during Frost's trial, so neither story was ever verified. Additionally, Samuel Upton — the man who would ultimately find Towne's body — would testify during the trial that he overheard Frost tell his (Upton's) wife that he (Frost) never did go to Worcester that day. But Upton's wife would testify that she understood Frost to say that he *had* gone to Worcester!

In the end, whether Frost was in Worcester that day or not, he *was away from the farm*, ostensibly to "meet up" with Towne, and going forward right up through his trial, that was to be Frost's story. The problem was, while his story was designed to end the talk about Frank's disappearance, it instead only fanned the flames. In fact, when Charles Rathbone returned to the farm on the 11th, he brought with him news of gossip flying in the neighboring towns of Dana, Hardwick, and Barre. The buzz was that a farmer in Petersham had murdered his brother-in-law. When Samuel heard that, he realized he had to take a more proactive approach if he was going to quell that gossip.

Step 2 - The Call For Help

As the rumors swirled, Frost tried as best he could to carry on with his farming. In fact, on July 10th Frost mowed a large parcel of land for one Alfred Peckham, a well-to-do farmer who lived some two miles north of Frost near the center of town. Peckham also just so happened to be on the Board of Selectman in Petersham at the time. Six days later on the 16th Peckham traveled down to the Frost farm to pay Samuel for the work he'd done. He found Frost working in his cabbage patch, and there the two men engaged in some generic banter prior to Peckham giving Frost his money. Peckham had heard the gossip around town just like everybody else, so before he left he nonchalantly asked, "So is Frank *gone*?" Frost was caught off guard by the question, but after gathering himself he responded, "Well, he is, he is gone, don't know when he'll be back." Peckham said, "Alright then, well, I'll let you know if I need any more mowing," and he headed home.

Peckham wasn't the only one curious about Frank. Strangers had started showing up at the Frost farm each evening wanting to see the place where the local man was rumored to have murdered his brother-in-law. As those visits increased, so did Frost's frustration with them. His exact quote on the matter was, "It ain't very pleasant." By July 20th Frost's aggravation had reached a boiling point, and so he decided to pay a visit to his new "friend" Alfred Peckham. Frost told Peckham about all the whispers and innuendo he'd heard about, and he complained loudly about the people who were lurking around his farm. Samuel then demanded that something be done about all of it. Peckham admitted that he too had heard the rumors, but he wasn't exactly sure what he was supposed to do about them. But Samuel had an idea. He suggested that Peckham publish a note in *The Barre Gazette* (the main newspaper in the town just south of Petersham), and he demanded that the note make it very clear that Frost had indeed seen Towne in Worcester on the 7th. Further, the note should state that Frost had sworn an oath to that effect. Peckham maintained a good poker face while listening to Frost's idea, but what Samuel didn't know was that Peckham was inclined to believe the rumors. So when Frost was done, Peckham sighed and then replied, "No, that won't do." He told Frost that before anything like that was going to happen, Frost would need to provide some sort of proof that Towne was still alive. If Frost could do that, Peckham said, then he would gladly revisit the matter. Frustrated with Peckham's response, Frost asked if they could go at once to see the Chairman of the Board of Selectmen about the situation. Peckham politely declined, but told Frost that he was free to do so on his own. Now visibly upset, Frost vowed to do just that, and he set off to speak with Peckham's boss, Joseph W. Upton.

    While Frost was acquainted with Peckham, he'd never met Upton. Thus, when he arrived unannounced at Upton's door, neither man knew what to expect from the other. Frost was hoping for a much more sympathetic and understanding ear, but he would not find one there. Frost would quickly learn that Sergeant Joseph W. Upton was not a man to be trifled with. Upton had served as Captain John Mudge's right hand man for the fabled 53rd Regiment of Massachusetts in the Civil War. (Mudge's portrait still hangs in the Petersham library.) Subsequently he had been chosen to chair the Board of Selectmen for several years running because he had *earned* the respect of the townsfolk. He was not the sort of man who could easily be made to play the fool. Frost introduced himself to the Chairman, and Upton asked what it was he could do for him. Samuel again sought help in dealing with the swirling rumors, and he pitched Upton on his newspaper note idea. Upton immediately scoffed at the thought, and like Peckham before him, he told Frost he needed to produce Towne if he was going to quiet the chatter. Frost wasn't going to give up easily, and so he began to recount his alleged interaction with Towne in Worcester on the 7th to bolster his case. Upton wanted no part of it however, and with a wave of his hand he cut Samuel off quickly. He stepped closer to Frost, looked him square in the eye, and said sternly, "Mr. Frost, if you killed that man, or injured him, you are aware of it!" It was the first time anyone had actually said those words to Samuel's face, and he was startled by it. But Frost responded firmly, "Kill him? He is my best friend. He was always there for me, he has always assisted me, and I him. We were the best of friends." Upton replied, "Mr. Frost, if that is so, then you must have some idea where your best friend is. You need to do whatever you can do to procure evidence of Mr. Towne's whereabouts." Frost told Upton, "He's most likely in California, but if he's not there then he's either in Grafton (Massachusetts) or up in Littleton (New Hampshire) with his parents." "You've got to locate him, Mr. Frost, and show everybody that he is alive and well," said Upton. Frost suggested that he could write letters to those areas to try and locate Frank. Upton loved the idea and he told Frost he should get to it immediately. He urged Frost to alert him as soon as he had any news, and then he bid him farewell. Frost thanked the Chairman for his time, and he vowed to see him again soon.

Now that he was boxed in by Upton, Frost felt he had no choice but to actually write those letters following their meeting. In fact, not only did he write FIVE letters — two to California, one to Grafton, and two to New Hampshire — he also stopped by Alfred Peckham's house on the way to the Post Office to show him the letters before he mailed them. Peckham would later testify that Frost read aloud one of the California letters at that time, as if to show Peckham just how serious he was about tracking Frank down. And after making the stop at Peckham's, Frost rode to the Post Office and actually mailed the letters out! Not surprisingly those letters would go unanswered, and Frost would not return to Upton's house as promised. But the two men would soon meet again, only this time it would be Upton showing up unannounced at Frost's farm.

Step 3 – The Moving of the Body

Frost was having increasing trouble with the Rathbone boys. Once Charles returned to the farm on the 11th, Samuel thought that he and John seemed to be doing a lot of snooping around. One of their daily chores was feeding the pigs, and the pigpen just so happened to be located under the barn about ten feet from where Towne's body lay. Frost sensed that the Rathbones were taking increasingly longer every time they went down to feed the pigs, and that was making him nervous. Additionally, Frost was starting to notice an unpleasant odor rising out of the ground where he'd buried Towne, and he wondered if the Rathbones might be noticing it too. (How bad must the smell have been that it could be detected despite its proximity to the pigpen?) When he first began to detect the odor, Frost had thought/hoped that it would soon go away, but instead it seemed to get stronger with each passing day. Frost decided he had to do something with the body.

Around 10:00pm on the night of July 22nd, Caroline Frost was resting in the north bedroom when she heard the kitchen door open and then close. Having grown highly suspicious of her husband by that point, she listened intently but did not hear anything for some time. But around midnight she heard what she thought was the thud of animal hooves, so she peered out the bedroom window just in time to see her husband's team of oxen heading out of the barn in the general direction of the swampy area behind the fields. About an hour later, she heard the oxen return to the barn. Then at approximately 2:00 am she heard the kitchen door open as her husband returned inside for the night. He did not join Carrie but instead went to the south bedroom to get just a few hours of sleep. (The two had not shared a bed since July 4th, Carrie would later testify, due to Samuel's choice.) She said nothing to her husband the next morning about what he'd been up to the previous night, but she had her suspicions.

Frost's timing could not have been better it turned out. Unbeknownst to him, the Rathbones had indeed been studying the rounded mound of fresh earth under the barn, and as the days had passed they began to notice the earth was starting to heave. (As gases were leaving Towne's body, they were causing the mound to shift upward.) After several days of wondering what was happening, seventeen-year-old John finally got up the nerve to find out. He took a rifle and poked the mound, and after the barrel of the gun had sunk in some three to four inches, the rifle sprang back at John. He repeated the action three more times, with the same startling result. The brothers had suspected something (or someone) was in there, but to be actually touching it was beyond alarming. After the last poke, the brothers covered their marks and then quickly left the barn. Not knowing what to do next, they sought out the advice of two trusted friends; John Belden, a neighbor who lived down the road towards Hardwick, and Abel Hastings of Dana. Hastings came to the farm the next day, Wednesday the 21st, and he too prodded the grave. He would later testify that when his stick bounced back on him, "A cold chill ran over me. I couldn't hardly stand, I was shivering, I was so kind of startled." The next morning (the 22nd) the Rathbones met up with Belden and Hastings, and they all agreed that it had to be Towne's body that was underneath the barn. Belden urged the Rathbones to seek out Chairman Upton for guidance, but the boys knew they couldn't do so that day without drawing Frost's attention. (Had they gone on the 22nd, things might well have turned out differently on the farm.) Instead the Rathbones went to Upton's house early on the morning of the 23rd (they too had never met him) and told him what they had discovered. Upton was not surprised, and he told the brothers that he would head down to the farm in short order to check things out for himself.

Upton had a few things to take care of at his house, but as soon as he finished he rode down to the Frost farm in his horse-drawn wagon with a young farmhand in tow. He dropped himself off about a quarter of a mile from the farm, and he told the farmhand to continue on into Hardwick and to take his time coming back for him. Upton then walked down to the farm unnoticed and went to the back of the barn. He quickly found the spot the Rathbones had described, grabbed a three-foot long stray board nearby, and poked the board into the soft part of the earth. Nothing. He poked again, and again the stick went two feet down with no resistance. Not quite satisfied, he found a long iron rod and sent it into the dirt lengthwise at an angle, but it too found nothing. He noted that the ground around the rectangular fresh sod was firm and solid, so he knew something *had been* at that spot, but whatever it was, it was now gone. Upton put the rod back and had a look around under the barn, but he saw nothing more out of the ordinary. Finding himself temporarily at a dead end, Upton stepped outside hoping to find the Rathbone boys.

Instead, as Upton stepped out from under the barn and turned the corner he came face to face with Samuel J. Frost, who was glaring right at him from just a few feet away. Whatever shivers had gone up Abel Hastings' spine two days prior were nothing compared to the lightning bolts of shock pulsing through Upton's body at that moment. As he stood there frozen in place, Frost calmly said, "Morning Mr. Upton, have you heard anything?" Frost must have been just as shocked to see the uninvited Upton as Upton was to see the unannounced Frost, but the murderer was playing it cool. Shaking off his initial panic Upton replied, "No, nothing new. You?" Without taking his eyes off Upton Frost said, "No, same." The two men stood there for what seemed an eternity just looking at one another until Frost again surprised Upton. "I wonder if you might come inside the house a minute since you're here," he said. Of course *that* was the last thing Upton wanted to do, but he was in a bit of a bind since his farmhand had not yet returned with the wagon. Now it was Upton trying to play it cool, and so after a long pause he said, "Sure, of course." As he walked several steps behind Frost to the house, Upton's mind was playing out several possible scenarios that might happen once he was inside.

Luckily, Upton's fears were quickly erased upon being greeted in the kitchen by a smiling Carrie Frost, who simply said, "Good morning" as if she'd been expecting him. Upton breathed a silent sigh of relief knowing that he was not to be alone with Samuel inside that house. The unpredictability of the day then continued, as the three of them then sat down in the parlor and casually conversed for some twenty minutes, "talking about nothing in particular" as Upton would later recall. At long last Upton's farmhand returned, and the Select-man's strange and scary visit to the Frost farm was almost over. But as he walked from the house towards his wagon, a steely Samuel yelled towards him, "You be sure to keep me posted if you hear anything." Without turning around Upton yelled back, "Indeed, likewise." Upton wondered if Frost was smiling at him in that moment, but he didn't look back. Upton was now positive that Frost had killed Towne, and he felt certain that this would not be his last visit to the farm.

Frost knew he had dodged a bullet by moving Towne's body the night before Upton's visit, but he also knew that *they* were now on to him. As a result, three days later on the 26th, as soon as Carrie put the children to bed at 8:00pm, Frost left the house and remained out *all night*. Carrie recalled hearing him come back into the house at three different times during that night, but each time he returned it was only for a minute or two, and then back out he went. When she awoke the next morning, she noticed three things. One, the butcher knife she kept on the kitchen windowsill was gone, and she specifically recalled seeing it there the night before. Two, a slop pail she also kept in the kitchen was missing. And three, her husband's pants were hanging outside on the clothesline, even though she'd just washed them the day before. When she checked to see why they were out there, she was met by an awful odor. (They smelled "like a dead body" she would later testify.) And when her husband awoke later that morning after getting very little sleep, he had that same dead body smell all over him too.

Samuel J. Frost had three missions following Towne's mur-der. First, he needed to convince people that Frank really had gone to California, but his Worcester story convinced *nobody* of that. Second, he hoped to garner support from some respected members in the community, but that effort went nowhere. Third, he had to make sure that Frank Towne's body was never found. After all, no body meant there would be no charges back in 1875 Massachusetts. But keeping the corpse hidden had proven difficult, and its detection had only been avoided by late nights and close calls. He'd been lucky, but his luck was about to run out, and soon Carrie wouldn't be the only one who'd have the misfortune of breathing in that "like a dead body" smell.

John Rathbone
(Photo courtesy of Orson Rathburn)

Pliny Henry Babbitt
(Photo courtesy of holcombgenealogy.com)

4

The Arrest

Frost made a fateful, and *fatal* as it would turn out, decision on the morning of Saturday, July 31st. He was having trouble keeping up with his farming (he'd been busy doing "other things" the last few weeks), and he needed help. He had asked George Josselyn to come back and work for him, but Josselyn felt uneasy about the idea and declined the offer. So Frost turned to his neighbor Samuel Upton, who lived a half mile south of Frost on Hardwick Road. (Samuel was no relation to Joseph W. Upton, Samuel was black, Joseph was white.) Frost had befriended Upton's wife after buying some cabbage plants from her, and she had mentioned to him that her husband was a skilled farm hand. Although he did not know Upton except in passing, Frost needed to get the rest of his (formerly Towne's) fields hayed. So he offered Upton the work, and Upton readily accepted. It was a decision Frost would live (and later die) to regret.

Initially the decision paid dividends, as Upton turned out to be exactly what Frost needed. He showed up promptly at 8:00am and worked straight through until 4:15pm in the hayfield on the north side of Frost's house. Upton hayed much of that field, and Frost was very pleased with the work. He would have been less pleased had he known that at some point during the day Charles Rathbone sought out Upton, and the two men discussed the mounting rumors swirling about the farm. Charles told Upton that he and his brother John had seen Frost digging around in the cornfield south of the house, which was strange because there was no need for Frost to have been there since the corn had been planted weeks ago. Upon heading home after his first day's work, Upton passed that very cornfield, and as he did so his curiosity got the best of him. He took a detour and had a look around, but he saw nothing out of the ordinary. But as he turned back towards the road, his eyes caught something peculiar in the southeast corner of that field. As he would later testify, "I saw this place that was, well, it was covered with bugs and flies." As he inched closer, "I saw, I called it at that time — I did not know what it was — a rug sticking out of the ground. I did not go near it." Instead, he made a mark on the stone wall to remind himself of the spot, and then he beat feet out of there.

As Upton continued south towards his home, he bumped into Daniel Belden and Charles Smith, who were chatting outside Belden's house. Belden had seen Upton working up at Frost's place, and he asked Upton how it went. Upton almost couldn't get the words out fast enough as he told the two men what he had just seen in the cornfield. Belden told him to go home, have dinner, and meet back at Belden's at 9:00pm. He also told Upton to bring anybody he could round up, as they could be in for a long night. When Upton returned promptly at 9:00, he had Frank and Augustus Upton in tow. Meanwhile Belden and Smith had assembled a small posse of their own. Henry Grover, Forrest Hicks, Luther Stone, German Legarre, Levi Hicks, and James Kildare were all there awaiting Upton's arrival. Petersham did not yet have a police force in 1875, so these men had been assembled in case Upton had indeed found Towne's body. After briefing the others on what he'd seen earlier, Upton grabbed his hoe and his lantern and he led the men north towards Frost's cornfield. It was a typically dark and quiet night in Petersham, except for the dozen men walking through the woods with lanterns and pitchforks hoping to find the buried body of a murdered man.

When the posse reached the stone wall, Upton searched for several minutes but he could not find the mark he'd left. But in spite of the mark's absence, he was able to locate the spot he was looking for because the ground where he had been just hours earlier was freshly turned over and it had been smoothed out. Only now there was no rug sticking out of the ground. The men worked the soil with the shovels, hoes and pitchforks they'd brought, but to no avail. There was nothing there except freshly turned earth. As Upton tried to convince every-body that he really had seen something there earlier, Henry Grover de-cided to bust Upton's chops, "There weren't nothing but a woodchuck buried there, and I think some dogs dug it up!" The men all laughed, and for a moment the tension in the field broke. But as they swung their lanterns away from the wall, they noticed some tracks headed in the direction of the nearby oat field. Levi Hicks and German Legarre followed the tracks into the field, and after a minute or so Hicks shout-ed back, "Over here!" The night suddenly went silent again as the col-lective tension of the group shot right back up. The moment of truth had finally arrived.

Lying in the middle of the oat field was *something*. It appeared to be a blanket or rug, and it seemed to be wrapped around something. It looked like it hadn't been there long, as the blanket (as it turned out to be) had a fair amount of fresh dirt all over it. Once everyone had gathered around, Levi Hicks took a deep breath, grabbed his hoe and rolled the mass over once and then twice so as to unwind the blanket. There was a sack inside, and as Hicks leaned in for a closer look he noticed something sticking out of that sack. He waved for a lantern to be brought closer, and when it was everybody's eyes shot wide open. Right there in front of them was a bone sticking some three inches or so out of the sack. Trying not to breathe (the stench was awful), Hicks bent down and took firm hold of the bundle with his left hand. Henry Grover knelt down next to him and slit the bag open with his hunting knife. Then Grover lifted his lantern high above the scene, and suddenly everything that had been rumored in town for so long had finally come to light.

There in that oat field, surrounded by a dozen men and several lanterns, was the body of Frank P. Towne... or, to be more exact, *some* of the body of Frank P. Towne. The men soon discovered that the sack contained only the middle third of Towne's decomposing corpse, starting at the lower chest area and ending at the upper thighs. The men gathered there had come to Frost's farm expecting to find a body, but they never imagined finding a *chopped up* body. They stood there in disbelief staring at the gruesome discovery for what seemed like an eternity. Finally someone said, "We'd better get Upton," and the reality of the situation suddenly kicked in.

The Upton in question was of course Joseph W. Upton, the Selectman who'd been taken by surprise when Samuel J. Frost knocked on his door just two weeks earlier. But this time the knock he heard on his door at 11:00 at night came as little surprise to him. After all, ever since he left the Frost farm the previous week he'd been expecting it. Once Luther Stone and German Legarre described what had just taken place at the Frost farm, Upton readied his horse for a ride down to Barre. He needed to fetch Sheriff Bothwell, the chief law enforcement officer for Barre, Hardwick, and Petersham. Upton told Stone and Legarre to alert Alfred Peckham as to the situation, and to inform Peckham that he was in charge at the farm until Upton returned with the sheriff. With that the three men quickly rode off into the night, knowing they would soon meet up again to arrest the man they'd long suspected of murder.

Peckham arrived at the farm around midnight. He was briefed, shown the torso, and tasked with keeping the men calm while they waited. They did so quietly until around 1:15am when out of nowhere the Frosts' dog started growling loudly inside the house and would not stop. After several minutes the men began to speculate as to why the dog was acting so strangely. Finally, around 1:30 or so, Upton and Bothwell arrived on the scene accompanied by Deputy Pliny Babbitt and the county coroner Henry Shattuck. Bothwell took one look at the weary men gathered at the farm and immediately got down to business. He announced that he and Babbitt were going to go inside the house and arrest Mr. Frost if he was there, and he instructed everyone else to spread out and surround the house in case Frost tried to flee. The sheriff then told Shattuck to personally watch the back door of the house, and as Shattuck began to head in that direction, he heard someone in the crowd pointedly ask in a non-joking manner, "Can we please shoot that dog?" No one in the crowd laughed, as they all thought it was a legitimate suggestion. Bothwell hadn't even noticed the dog however, and he ignored the request. Instead, he asked if anyone there was familiar with the layout of the house. Jairus Williams said he was, and Bothwell signaled for Williams to join him and Babbitt as they headed towards the kitchen door.

When they got there, Bothwell gently rapped on the door but he heard no response. He rapped again, and then a third time, but still he heard nothing. He looked over at Williams, who pointed to a window on the left and told Bothwell that the Frosts slept in that room. Bothwell nodded to Babbitt, who was closest to that window, and Babbitt tapped on it. Suddenly a female voice could be heard over the now barking dog.

"What do you want?" Caroline Frost asked.

"We are going to need you to open the door, ma'am," Babbitt replied.

"One minute," she responded.

Within a matter of seconds, the front door opened. Bothwell exchanged no greeting with Mrs. Frost, but instead moved quickly past her and headed into the bedroom. Not seeing the man he was looking for in there, Bothwell addressed Mrs. Frost.

"Where's your husband ma'am?" Bothwell demanded.

"I can't tell you." Caroline responded.

"Is he in the house?" Bothwell's impatience was palpable.

"I don't know." Caroline responded louder this time, as she did not like Bothwell's tone.

Bothwell shook his head as he stormed past Mrs. Frost. He proceeded to the dining room, then the parlor, and finally the south bedroom, but there was no sign of Frost. Looking at the staircase leading up out of the south bedroom, Bothwell again glanced at Babbitt and nodded. Babbitt nodded in return, and the two men slowly ascended the stairs. The Rathbones' bedroom (Towne's old room) was to their left, and it was empty. But as they turned back to their right, they both noticed a silhouette, and it was moving ever so slightly. Tucked in behind an old loom in the attic was Petersham's Public Enemy #1. Bothwell spoke, "Come on out Mr. Frost," and a nervous Samuel did as instructed. Bothwell identified himself as a Deputy Sheriff of Worcester County and he handcuffed Frost. He and Babbitt then each took an arm of their prisoner and carefully led him down the stairs. After sitting him down in the parlor, Bothwell called out for Shattuck to come inside, and he told the coroner to bring a couple of men with him. It was going to be their job to watch over Frost and protect him from the men outside.

With Frost secured, Bothwell and Babbitt stepped out to see what had been found of Frank Towne firsthand. After a quick look inside the sack (the putrid smell kept the inspection brief), Bothwell ordered Levi Hicks to bring the body and the blanket up to the barn, which he did with the help of a Mr. Blackmere. The sheriff told the two men to stand guard over the evidence until further notice, and he then signaled to Babbitt and new arrival Leander Hathaway to follow him back to the house. Once inside, Bothwell ordered Frost to change his clothes because, as Babbitt would later testify, Samuel had about him "a stench that was unbearable, and it was precisely the same as the body" they had just inspected. When Frost returned to the parlor, Hathaway sat down to his right and Babbitt sat to his left. It was time to talk to the suspect, and Babbitt was the man Bothwell picked to do the questioning.

Pliny Henry Babbitt was an auctioneer by trade, and as such he made his living in part by getting people to do things (bid higher) that they didn't necessarily want to do. At 58, he was also the oldest in the group (Bothwell was 47, Hathaway was only 37). He had a long history in law enforcement, having been the Deputy Sheriff himself long before Bothwell's arrival, and he had served as a constable since 1866. (Bothwell meanwhile had only been the Deputy Sheriff for a year and a half.) The thinking was that if Frost was going to say anything, the veteran Babbitt was the man to get him to do so. Pliny put his right hand on

Frost's left knee, and using his calm voice he began.

"Mr. Frost, do you know what we're here for?"

Frost drew in a deep breath and replied softly, "I suppose I do."

"For what are we here for Mr. Frost?" Babbitt responded.

Frost wasn't biting. "I don't wish to say nothing about that," he replied.

"Mr. Frost, we have found part of the body, and it is only a matter of time in regard to the rest, you would do us a great deal and do us a great kindness if you would tell us where the rest is." Babbitt was being as fatherly as he could as he played "good cop", but Frost said nothing as he blankly stared ahead.

"You could really help us, Mr. Frost." Babbitt repeated, but again Frost stayed silent.

"Where is the rest of the body Mr. Frost?" Babbitt pleaded, careful to make his voice softer with each asking.

Frost finally responded, "I can't tell you."

"Do you have anything to say about that?" Babbitt inquired quizzically.

Frost shook his head. "I have not. I have nothing to say."

"I have to ask Mr. Frost," Babbitt persisted, "Did you feed the rest to the hogs, or has maybe the dog eaten it?"

Frost snapped back, "The dog hasn't eaten anything." It was the first and only time Frost raised his voice with Babbitt.

"Do you have anything to say about the body, anything Mr. Frost?" Babbitt's tone was much more forceful this time.

Frost gruffly retorted, "I have not. I have nothing to say." Frost sat back in the couch signaling that for now, he was done talking. Pliny looked at Bothwell and shook his head, as he knew the moment had passed and there was no point in continuing.

The sheriff asked Babbitt to take the lead in searching for more evidence around the farm. He directed Hathaway to relieve Hicks in guarding the torso in the barn. He then asked Shattuck to accompany him as he took Frost to the jail in Barre. But as the two men led the prisoner outside, Shattuck stated that he would need to return to the farm once Frost was locked up, in case more of Towne's body was found. The problem was, Shattuck didn't have his horse at Frost's farm because he had ridden up with Bothwell in the two-person wagon. The men were stymied as they tried to figure out how Shattuck would return. Then the unexpected happened. *Frost* broke the silence, "You can just use my horse." Sure enough, Shattuck took Frost up on the offer, and he rode the prisoner's horse all the way to the jail and then back again.

It was on that seven-mile journey that Bothwell decided to take his shot at questioning Frost, although Samuel was the one who initially broke the silence.

"I can't tell you how relieved I was when you told me you was the law. I thought you might be one of them men outside come to get me, and I knew that wasn't going to be good."

Bothwell let Frost's statement linger for a second before he took the conversation in a different direction.

"So how did you come to kill Frank?"

Taken aback, Frost said, "I got nothing to say about it."

"Well the Selectman told me that the last place you saw Frank was in Worcester, is that correct?" Bothwell was already in full-interrogation mode.

"I did."

"And you settled with him there?"

"I did. I paid him some money and gave him a note for the rest."

"Where did you meet him exactly?"

"We met down on Front Street, below the park in a shop."

"What kind of shop was it?"

"It was a saloon, down on the right."

"Which one exactly? Who owned it?"

"I don't know," said Frost.

"Did you write the note in the saloon?"

"I did."

"Where'd you get the paper?"

"I got it off the bartender in the saloon. "

"Pen and ink too?"

"Yes sir."

"And where in the saloon did you write the note?"

"I wrote it on a showcase in there."

"Where was the showcase? Was it directly ahead of you as you walked in to the saloon, or was it to your right or your left?"

"It was on the left side."

"And where did you get the paper?"

"I had it with me."

"And you told the Selectman that Frank went to California. Did you see him get on the train that day?"

"He said he was going to California on the 5:00pm train, and I just assumed he got on it."

The cat and mouse game between the two men was getting Bothwell nowhere, and he was getting more and more agitated as Frost insisted on continuing with the fictitious Worcester story. Bothwell had caught him changing his answer on the "where did you get the paper" question, and by the time Frost made the 5:00pm train comment, Bothwell was about ready to unload on him. He clenched his teeth and glared at the side of Frost's face as he asked him one last thing.

"So how do you suppose Frank got all the way back from California and up into that corn field without any legs?"

The line was designed to be a shocking "end of conversation" rhetorical question, delivered with the utmost disdain. But the question wasn't rhetorical, and Samuel's response to it was equally shocking. Rather than snap back at Bothwell (as he had when Pliny Babbitt asked about the dog), Frost instead burst out laughing! While Bothwell's question was loaded with contempt, Frost instead picked up on the unintended dark humor in it, and he cackled so loudly that Coroner Shattuck (riding behind them on Frost's horse) wondered what had actually happened. And when Samuel's laughter temporarily subsided, he looked directly at Bothwell and as the two men locked eyes, Frost chuckled and said gleefully,

"You know, I don't know!"

He then turned away from the sheriff, gently shaking his head and chuckling as he did so. The sheriff also shook his head as he too turned away, but he wasn't laughing.

With that, the conversation ended. It was almost four o'clock in the morning and the men were fast approaching their destination, the Barre jail. The strange night had started with Henry Grover laughing at Samuel Upton, and it was now ending with Samuel Frost laughing at Sylvester Bothwell. But there was nothing funny about what had transpired in the six hours between those two laughs. Franklin P. Towne was now officially dead, and two-thirds of his body was still missing. Samuel J. Frost was soon to be sitting in a jail cell having been arrested for his brother-in-law's murder. And Carrie Frost sat in her bedroom trying to figure out how she was going to tell her four children why their father would no longer be at home. It was as strange a night as the quiet little town of Petersham had ever seen. The next morning would be no less so.

Sheriff Sylvester Bothwell
(As printed in *The Boston Globe* on August 24, 1902)
(Courtesy of newspapers.com)

EASTERN SPECIALS.

THE PETERSHAM TRAGEDY— FROST LODGED IN JAIL.

Mr. Beecher's Triumphant Arrival at His Summer Parish.

Reopening of the Hearing on the Vermont Central Railroad.

Suicide at Montpelier—Odd Fellows' Celebration—The Fall River Labor Troubles— The Mills Closed.

Page 3 headline in the *Boston Daily Globe* on August 4, 1875
(Courtesy of newspapers.com)

5

The Day After

Samuel J. Frost had finally been removed from his home on Hardwick Road, but everyone else who'd been there since nightfall remained. While the suspect was now under arrest, there was still much work to be done on the farm if they were going to prove he was indeed the killer. Coroner Shattuck returned as dawn approached, and he was greeted by a bevy of weary men, many of whom hadn't slept in over twenty-four hours. Their first priority was to try and figure out the exact cause of Towne's death, because Sheriff Bothwell needed that in order to determine what the specific charges for Frost would be. Meanwhile, J.W. Upton wanted to secure as much evidence as possible while the crime scene was still fresh. And Pliny Babbitt was hoping to talk to Mrs. Frost before she'd had a chance to fully process everything that had happened. So there was plenty to do and time was of the essence, so sleep would simply have to wait.

As soon as dawn broke, Upton gathered together a posse and announced that their assignment was to find the rest of the body. Frank Towne's torso had proved that he was indeed dead, but it gave no clues as to how he'd met his demise. Charles Rathbone spoke up and stated that he and his brother had seen Frost digging in the cornfield over the past few nights. Upton looked at John Rathbone, who nodded confirmation of his brother's claim. It was as good a spot to start as any, so Upton waved his arm forward and the group headed off in that direction. Once there, Upton placed the men side by side and then slowly marched them forward with their heads down. When the line had gone about six rods into the cornfield (100 feet or so), Pliny Babbitt's voice broke the quiet of the morning. "Found something," he yelled, and the line immediately came to a stop. Just a few feet in front of Babbitt was what appeared to be fresh earth, and it seemed to be *moving*. As J.W. Upton would later testify, that spot in front of Babbitt was "something that scented very bad, and the worms were crawling out of the ground, back and forth." That "very bad scent" was one Upton and his men had become all too familiar with over the past several hours, but several of them covered their mouths just the same.

Seventeen-year-old John Rathbone stepped forward with a shovel, and after confirming that this was the area where he'd recently seen Frost, he started digging. The earth was loose and easy to move, and as Rathbone dug down, a feeling of déjà vu quickly swirled around the men. Sure enough, he unearthed a blanket wrapped around a large object maybe a foot or so down. As Rathbone pulled it up and then opened it, all the tired eyes opened wide as they gazed upon the decomposing chest, shoulders, and head of Frank Towne. It was precisely what the men had set out to find, but they were nonetheless stunned by their macabre discovery.

After several moments of shocked silence, Upton and Babbitt stepped closer for a better look. They quickly noticed three important things. One, the upper torso still had a blue shirt covering it, which the Rathbones identified as Towne's. Two, the decomposition of the head was nearly complete, making any facial identification impossible. As Shattuck would later testify, "There was no hair or flesh on the skull or the face, and there was a dampness to the skull, and in the eye sockets there was a sort of fleshy mass in there." Third and most importantly, the men noticed that the skull had a caved-in hole located behind the right ear. Shattuck knew the significance of that fracture instantly. He turned to Upton and told him that he would be ready to hold his official inquest in very short order. Upton promised to assemble a jury to assist Shattuck in evaluating all the evidence they'd gathered. Then Shattuck asked Babbitt to assist him in taking the head and shoulders to the barn, while Upton ordered the rest of the men to continue the search for the remaining portion of Towne's body. However, despite their best efforts — and as Henry Grover would later testify, "there were hundreds of people there, scouring that cornfield" — they were unable to locate the lower third of Towne's body. In fact, his legs would never be found.

While the men searched, Babbitt and Shattuck were making their way to the barn when Shattuck decided to take a detour. Although the two men were 100% certain as to whose head and shoulders they were carrying, Shattuck thought that a positive identification from a relative might more easily satisfy the law. So the two men carried the stinking sack with them past the barn up to the kitchen door of the house. Then, after looking at each other with expressions that said 'here goes nothing,' they knocked. A tired Carrie Frost was inside preparing breakfast for her children when she heard the knock and she

thought to herself, "*Now what?*" Upon opening the door she was greeted by *that* smell, and she immediately turned her head. As she tried
not to breathe, Shattuck spoke. "Mrs. Frost, I am so sorry to do this
to you right now, but we have found the top portion of your brother's
body in the field out back, and we were hoping that you could confirm
for us that it is indeed your brother. Do you think you could do that
for us?"

Carrie couldn't quite believe what she was being asked to do.
After all, her husband had just been arrested for murder, there were
currently hundreds of people searching in a field outside of her house,
and she'd hardly slept at all in the last twenty-four hours. All she
wanted to do that morning was keep her children as sheltered from the
situation as possible. Yet here she was now being asked to identify her
brother's worm-infested corpse as she tried to make breakfast for her
family. She pondered the request in disbelief for several seconds before
softly nodding her head.

"Thank you, Mrs. Frost," Shattuck said as Babbitt opened the
sack. Carrie's eyes glanced down for the briefest of moments, and then
she looked right back at Shattuck and said, "That's him."

"Thank you, Mrs. Frost," the coroner replied. He paused for
a moment, then said, "I apologize again Ma'am, but for the record,
we need to know how you can be so sure this is your brother." Carrie
sighed, "The skull. Its shape, it's like my brother's."

Shattuck needed more, and as uncomfortable as it was to ask,
he did. "Is there anything more recognizable? Perhaps you could take
a second look." Carrie's eyes stared at Shattuck's. She had no intention
of looking inside the sack a second time, and she didn't. Instead, as she
kept her eyes locked on Shattuck she offered, "The teeth. Frank's teeth
stood out. They were somewhat crowded so that they stood out prom-
inently."

"That sounds right, although some of his front teeth have been
smashed in," Shattuck said, not realizing just how jarring his words
would be to Mrs. Frost until after he'd said them. But instead of Carrie's
eyes filling with tears, Shattuck noticed her jaw clench. In that moment
Carrie realized exactly what her husband had done to her brother, and
a rush of disgust and hatred swelled up inside of her.

"His eye teeth are shaped very distinctly too, and they are rather
yellow," she said, a little more softly this time.

Babbitt closed up the sack and gave Shattuck's elbow a tug. He
knew they had more than enough confirmation and it was time to let

Carrie return to her children. Shattuck said, "Mrs. Frost, we can't thank you enough, you have been extremely helpful. We are very sorry to have had to do show you this. Thank you."

"That's my brother in there, and you *know* that's my brother in there." Hostility oozed out of Carrie's every word, and Shattuck sensed an opportunity. "Mrs. Frost, we are going to be holding an official inquest into your brother's death in just a short time, might you be able to spare a few minutes to tell those men what you just told us?"

"Yes, I can," Carrie said resolutely, nodding as she did.

"Thank you, Mrs. Frost. We will come get you when we are ready."

Carrie watched as Shattuck and Babbitt turned to head for the barn. She felt an urge to follow them right then and there, but she did have the kids' breakfast still to finish. As she closed the kitchen door she strangely felt like a huge weight had been lifted off her shoulders. She no longer had to tiptoe around the husband she'd been so suspicious of for the last month, and she now knew exactly what had happened. The knowledge had both saddened and enraged her, but at least it would now be out in the open, and that was a relief.

Back inside the barn, Babbitt handed his sack to Leander Hathaway and told him to keep it with the torso. J.W. Upton had also made his way back to the barn, and the two discussed what to do next. Upton decided that the area under the barn (where he had been only ten days earlier) needed a more thorough searching. He grabbed Jairus Williams and a couple of shovels, and together they went to sift through the original grave. (Had Upton done so ten days ago, he most likely would have been able to arrest Frost then, as he would soon find out.) Once the two men began turning over the loose earth under the barn, Upton quickly found what appeared to be a thumbnail. A minute later he found two hard, thick pieces of skin "which appeared as though they might have come off the bottom of a foot, the heel," as Upton would later testify. There was no question that Towne's body had been in that location at one point, and Upton shook his head knowing that he should have been more thorough ten days earlier.

Meanwhile, Babbitt, Shattuck, and the newly arrived Dr. George Brown were carefully scouring the main floor of the barn for evidence. Near one of the stalls where the cows were kept Babbitt noticed what appeared to be blood stains on the floor. Shattuck then pointed to blood on both the stanchion surrounding the stall and on the sill of the window there. Thinking this spot might well be the main crime scene, they moved to gather some of that blood as evidence. Dr. Brown found an axe in the barn and said he would chop out the stains. But Shattuck was concerned that in so doing, Brown might miss and actually destroy the evidence. So Babbitt looked around until he found what looked to be an iron hammer, although a large chunk of it had been broken off. Little did he know then but the missing chunk was actually the murder weapon. Babbitt had Dr. Brown hold the axe as a wedge while he struck the axe with the hammer. In so doing they were able to chip out several chunks of blood-soaked wood.

Sheriff Bothwell finally arrived back on scene and asked the men to brief him on the developments. Babbitt told him about the discovery of the top part of the body, which caused Bothwell to nod affirmatively, and Upton produced the rotted heel flesh, which caused Bothwell to wince. The sheriff thought for a moment and then asked the two men if they would join him in inspecting the lane behind the barn. They did, and almost immediately they noticed several stones along the path had been overturned, as if something large had been dragged over them causing them to flip. Several of those stones had what appeared to be human hair clinging to them. Then during the return trip to the barn they fanned out, which led Upton to discover a blanket and a hatchet behind the stone wall to the right of the lane.

They'd collected a treasure trove of evidence at that point, and Bothwell sensed that the men were quickly approaching exhaustion. He rhetorically asked Shattuck if he was ready to begin his inquest and then inquired if Upton had been able to assemble the needed "jury" to assess and ratify the coroner's findings. Upton had. He chose himself, along with Alfred Peckham, S.D. Goddard (he'd been Chairman of the Selectmen prior to Upton's tenure), Jairus Williams, George Ayers, Elijah Hildreth, and Colonel Josiah White, who was asked to be jury foreman. These men had two jobs: one, to confirm that Shattuck's cause of death was accurate, and two, to ensure that there was enough evidence to hold Frost, pending an official indictment. For most of these men, it would be both the first and last time they were ever involved in a murder case.

The inquest started in the barn around 9:00am, mere feet from where the actual crime was committed. Carrie Frost was summoned, and she was asked to tell the jury whatever she thought pertinent. She did not hold back. She revealed everything she knew of July 4th on the farm, and stated she had been suspicious of her husband almost immediately. After Samuel's alleged Worcester visit, she noticed her husband had both her brother's pocket watch and his knife, although there was no reason for him to have them in his possession. She then offered that since her brother's disappearance, her husband had been outside late at night on several occasions. She specifically recalled the night of the 26th, when she had heard the team of oxen go by, as well as the morning of the 27th when she found her husband's stink-filled overalls hanging on her clothesline. Finally, she told the men something they hadn't yet heard from her: that she remembered seeing her carving knife on the windowsill in the kitchen during the evening of the 26th, but on the morning of the 27th that knife was gone.

Had there been any doubts about where Carrie Frost's allegiance would be — with her brother or with her husband — those doubts were removed in the barn on August 1st. She had laid out the case against her husband in a way that no one else could, complete with a timeline of suspicious activity. And following her testimony, Carrie stayed in the barn while the men examined Towne's remains. She repeated for the jury that based on the hair, teeth, and shape of the skull, the victim was indeed her brother. She also confirmed that the blue shirt on the upper torso belonged to Frank. She told them *everything*.

As a formality, the jury quickly examined the rest of the evidence gathered — blankets, hair, axes, decomposing flesh. Then Shattuck brought out Towne's skull and pointed to the gaping hole below the ear. He explained that this was the blow that had led directly to Towne's death. Colonel White suddenly spoke up, "I think we've seen more than enough, yes gentlemen?" Everyone in the barn agreed. The colonel then stated for the record, "Franklin P. Towne came to his death Sunday, July 4th, by reason of a fracture in his skull inflicted by Samuel J. Frost. Even though the manner in which the blow was struck is as yet unknown, the jury feels that there is overwhelming evidence to justify charging Mr. Frost with the murder of Mr. Towne." That ended the official Coroner's Inquest.

Bothwell thanked everyone for their tremendous work over the past twelve hours, and he then sent them home. It was Sunday after all, and these men had church services to attend, just as they had on the fateful morning of July 4th. Bothwell asked only Upton, Babbitt, and Shattuck to remain, as he wanted to walk the grounds one more time just to make sure they hadn't missed anything. The case was beyond solid already, but one thing was nagging at Bothwell: Where were Towne's legs? He knew the men had been over and over the corn field, so he wanted to double-check the swampy area behind that field.

It proved to be a wise decision, as not long after they got out there they found what appeared to be another freshly dug grave. The men removed nearly two feet of soil before they struck something hard. After removing as much loose dirt as possible, they realized they'd hit upon a rock ledge. Upon closer examination, they realized the ledge had scrape marks all over it. There was also a large partially-hacked tree root running through the ledge. Towne's legs weren't there, but clearly Frost had unwisely attempted to put something there recently. Bothwell asked Upton to go over the spot with a fine-toothed comb, and Upton found several broken buttons — brown buttons with black streaks in them — that seemed to match the buttons on Towne's blue shirt. (The shirt that his upper torso was still wearing was indeed missing several buttons.)

Bothwell wasn't done. After walking the perimeter of the property and coming up empty, he found himself standing at the front entrance of the barn. As he stood there wondering if he might have missed anything, he began to take note of the stone wall across the street. Just to be sure, he decided to take a quick look. He crossed the street and paced back and forth in front of the wall, but he saw nothing unusual. Noticing some cut wood piled behind the wall (cord wood length), he leaned over the wall and took a peak. And there it was, the murder weapon. "It lay upon some wood in the ground. I found that piece of iron lying upon the ground between some logs of apple tree wood. It was not concealed in any way." Bothwell knew instantly what he was now holding in his hand.

The sheriff quickly returned to the barn to share his find with the others. They all agreed as to the significance of the find, and Shattuck suggested that maybe it was now time to break for the day. But Bothwell desperately wanted to find those legs, and so he insisted that they examine underneath the barn one last time before they went home. So Shattuck checked the interiors of several barrels that were in the cellar while Babbitt started reaching his hand into several large holes in the stone foundation of the barn on the south east side. Sure enough, Babbitt felt something strange inside one of those holes. He pulled his arm out, and in his hand was a large wallet and chain. The wallet contained several papers belonging to Towne, including an IOU from Frost to Towne for $325. The chain appeared to go with Towne's pocket watch. Bothwell surmised that Towne had the items on him when Frost killed him. The sheriff guessed that Frost must have hastily hidden them in the wall right before he buried Towne's body, only to forget about them in all the excitement. Bothwell's extra searches hadn't produced Towne's legs, but they had been invaluable nonetheless.

Bothwell knew that the men were now running on fumes, and although he hadn't found Towne's legs, he reluctantly agreed to call it a day. The only thing left was the final treatment of Towne's remains. The sheriff asked Babbitt to secure and preserve Towne's shirt for evidence, which he did with the help of Dr. Brown, who carefully unbuttoned the shirt and removed it from the corpse. Babbitt placed it in a pail of water to somewhat subdue the stench, knowing that the shirt was going to accompany him on his return trip to Barre. (He gave the shirt a thorough washing later that day when he got home.) Babbitt laid Towne's shoulders next to the torso on the barn floor and then arranged the skull on top of the shoulders like they were puzzle pieces. He and Brown wrapped the body parts in a sheet and placed the remains inside a coffin that Upton had hastily ordered in the middle of the night, along with a headstone, at a cost of $50 to the town. Upton then entrusted the coffin to Joseph Moore, who rode a mile up the road to the South cemetery, where Thomas Aldrich, the town's sexton (grave digger) was waiting. At 4:00pm that Sunday afternoon, Aldrich laid two-thirds of Franklin P. Towne down in his *final* resting place.

It had been just twenty-four hours since Samuel Upton first spotted the "rug" sticking out of the dirt near the stone wall on his way home. But those twenty-four hours had been perhaps the busiest in the history of quiet little Petersham. The townsfolk were already buzzing over what had happened in that time, and within the next twenty-four hours, the rest of the country would be too. As a result of what happened on that farm in those twenty-four hours, Samuel J. Frost and Petersham would both soon be famous.

ter's course in Leominster are Vice President Wilson, Gen. Kilpatrick, John B. Gough, Bishop Haven and Dr. G. C. Lorrimer.

Next Friday the Catholics of Oxford will have a picnic at the grove of George Hodges, Esq., to celebrate the centennial of Daniel O'Connell's birth. Major McCafferty of Worcester is expected to deliver an address on the occasion. A special train will be run from Webster.

The body of Fred. P. Towne of Petersham, who has been missing since July 4th, was found yesterday in a field two miles from his home. The limbs were missing, and other mutilations point to murder. L. J. Frost, a brother-in-law, has been arrested on suspicion.

The gold and silver mine which has been found on Mr. Chamberlain's farm, on the edge of Sturbridge, is now in a fair way for being worked, as Mr. Chamberlain set three men to work on it last Monday. The last specimen rock which he sent to Boston in order to be tested yielded gold and silver at the rate of $36 to the ton.

The dedication of Cushing Academy in Ashburnham occurs Tuesday, September 7th, and the school will be opened on the following day with a fair number of pupils. The academy has secured the services of Prof. James E. Vose, principal of the Francestop N. H. academy as

The first mention of the crime in any newspaper.
(As printed in *The Worcester Daily Spy* on August 2, 1875)

San Francisco Chronicle.

SAN FRANCISCO, CAL., SATURDAY, AUGUST 28, 1875.

A THRILLING TRAGEDY.

AN ATROCIOUS CRIME IN PETER-SHAM, MASSACHUSETTS.

A Farmer Kills His Brother-in-Law and Chops Him to Pieces—How the Murder Came to Light.

[From the Springfield Republican, August 3d.]

The circumstances attending the murder of Frank P. Towne of Petersham, who has been missing since July 4th, and whose concealed body was discovered in a terribly mutilated condition on Sunday, form the most remarkable story of crime almost in the history of this region; for it is now found beyond doubt that the the murderer is Sam. J. Frost, brother-in-law of the dead man. The scene of the murder was a farm about three miles south of Petersham Center, and about twelve miles from Athol. The murdered man leased this farm from Frost last Spring, and engaged Frost and his wife to live with him and help carry on the place. The men had lived quietly and pleasantly, for aught that is known, until Sunday morning, July 4th, when Frost and Towne went out to the barn to milk and do the chores. It is supposed that during the altercation Frost struck Towne with a stone-hammer, as the

SKULL WAS FOUND TO BE CRUSHED IN

A little above and behind the right ear, at least three inches square. Soon after having done the deed, Frost returned to the house with one pail full of milk and another empty. In reply to the inquiries of his wife as to where her brother was, Frost said he and Frank had a quarrel, and he gave him a black eye, and Frank had gone away. She, thinking no more about it, went away to church. On her return, as Towne did not appear, she again inquired where he was, and Frost answered that he had gone to Worcester, after having sold to him the stock and crops of the farm, where he was to meet Frank on Tuesday. When Tuesday came she asked her husband if they were going to Worcester, to which he replied that he had agreed to go either Tuesday or Wednesday. On Wednesday he went, and brought on his return a new suit of clothes, and said Towne had gone to California, he (Frost) having given him $150 in money and his note for $175. After his return from Worcester, his wife says that Frost changed his sleeping-room, and would often get up and go out, and be gone a large portion of the night; a week ago yesterday he was gone all night—as is supposed, to conceal the body. About this time she missed a carving-knife and pail, and asked Frost if he had seen them; but he

6

The Newspapers

The world first heard of Samuel J. Frost and Frank P. Towne on Monday, August 2nd, 1875, when the *Worcester Daily Spy* ran a tiny item in their "County News" column. Sandwiched between mentions of an upcoming Catholic picnic in Oxford and a silver find in Sturbridge was the following:

> The body of Fred. P. Towne of Petersham, who has been missing since July 4th, was found yesterday in a field two miles from his home. The limbs were missing, and other mutilations point to murder. L. J. Frost, a brother-in-law, has been arrested on suspicion.

Towne and Frost were such unknowns that the paper got both of their names wrong. Further, the field where two-thirds of Towne's body had been recovered was not "two miles from his home," it was closer to a quarter of a mile away (as Carrie would later testify). Still, this was the first taste of Frost-Towne for the people of Worcester County.

But this story wasn't just news in Central Massachusetts. That exact item was also published in both *The Baltimore Sun* and *The Philadelphia Inquirer* that same day. An enhanced version appeared in the evening edition of *The Burlington Free Press and Times*, which had it as the second item in the "New England News" column:

> A MURDER DISCOVERED –
> ARREST OF THE PROBABLE MURDERER.
> On the 4th ult. Frederick P. Towne, a well-to-do farmer living near Petersham, Mass, suddenly disappeared, and his brother-in-law, J. Frost, announced that he had gone to California, and left his property in his charge. No general suspicions of foul play were entertained until yesterday, when the mutilated body of the missing man was found in a field adjoining the farm. It is known that Towne and Frost had a quarrel on the morning of

the 4th ult., and for this and other reasons the latter is thought to be the guilty man. Frost was arrested yesterday and is now confined awaiting the results of the investigation.

The *Free Press* added to the original version that Towne was a "well-to-do farmer"; he most certainly was not. They also had both names wrong, referring to one as "J. Frost" and the other as "Frederick" Towne. And there had been plenty of "suspicions of foul play" in and around the farm prior to Frost's arrest, contrary to the article. But the essence of the story was accurate, and word of the events in Petersham was clearly spreading fast.

While the news had started to percolate on August 2nd, it exploded on August 3rd. That's because while those two error-laced items were popping up in a few newspapers on the 2nd, Frost was making his initial court appearance that day as well, and the media were there. It was a simple evidentiary hearing before Judge Edwin Woods in Barre, who naturally found that there was more than enough evidence to hold Frost until he could appear before a grand jury in Fitchburg Superior Court the following week. The judge also ordered Sheriff Bothwell to deliver Frost immediately to the Worcester County Jail, which he did that evening. Interestingly, Bothwell would later report that Frost was very chatty during that ride, and he made a point of noting that Frost had expressed relief about getting further away from Petersham.

When Samuel woke up in the Worcester County Jail on the morning of the 3rd, he was on his way to becoming a household name. While Judge Woods' hearing had been entirely ordinary from a legal standpoint, it was beyond extra-ordinary from a newsman's perspective. After all, it was in that hearing where the first public account of Frost's crime was given, and that account had much more detail than those two August 2nd items. As a result, the next day's newspapers ran wild with all the gruesome particulars. *The Worcester Daily Spy* ran a three-column story on page 1 under the headline:

The Petersham Murder.
A Horrible Crime and Desperate
Attempt to Escape Detection.

The first line of the column that followed set the tone for newspaper sensationalism everywhere:

The usually quiet country town of Petersham was thrown into a state of intense excitement Sunday morning by the announcement that a most diabolical murder had been committed within the town limits.

Gone was the mere regurgitation of "facts", now *The Spy's* writers were putting all their energies into making the story sizzle. The rest of that article was titillating, transfixing, and 100% true.

Meanwhile, *The Athol Transcript's* feature story began this way:

PETERSHAM.
A MYSTERY CLEARED UP –
Discovery of the Mutilated Remains of a Murdered Man –
ONE OF THE MOST ATROCIOUS MURDERS ON RECORD.

And while Frost didn't make the front page of the Boston papers on August 3rd, he did garner an entire column on page 4 of *The Boston Post*, which began with this understatement:

The normal quiet of Petersham, in Worcester County, is just now disturbed by the discovery of what appears to have been a tragedy of no ordinary character.

"Diabolical," "atrocious," "of no ordinary character"… the people of Massachusetts were suddenly finding out that something exceedingly wicked had taken place in their state. And they were fascinated by it.

Note that the writer for the Boston paper felt the need to point out where Petersham was geographically! It was that very uncertainty which would put the town onto *The Boston Post's* front page two days later. In a peculiar column titled "All Sorts", which contained random one-sentence thoughts ranging from, "Nice plums in Jersey and plenty of 'em," to "The Vice President is taking white sulphur," the following line appeared:

Much obliged to Mr. Frost for letting us know that there's such a town as Petersham.

Samuel J. Frost and his misdeeds had literally put Petersham on the map for people outside of Worcester County. Those readers wouldn't soon forget it either, as Frost's case would appear on pages 1 or 2 of *The*

Boston Post more than a dozen times over the next ten months.

And interest in the story was hardly limited to Massachusetts. While it was certainly unusual for Petersham to find itself on the front page of a Boston newspaper (then or now), it was seemingly impossible for it to be on the front page of a newspaper 3000 miles away in California. (It had never happened before, nor has it happened since.) But sure enough, on August 28th, 1875, the front page of *The San Francisco Chronicle* splashed the following:

A THRILLING TRAGEDY.
AN ATROCIOUS CRIME IN
PETERSHAM, MASSACHUSETTS.

By the time Frost's story had made it's way to the West Coast, it had already turned up on the front page of *The St. Louis Post Dispatch* on August 5th under the headline "The Petersham Murder". That same day *The New York Sun* published a lengthy feature titled "The Petersham Mystery: A Murder By An Avaricious Brother-In-Law". *The Pittsburgh Daily Gazette* of August 6th had shocked its readers with the headline, "A Man Chopped Up and Buried By His Brother-in-Law." And the front page of Virginia's *The Bristol News* on August 17th had the story with a bold block letter headline that simply said, "**MURDER!**"

Perhaps the best headline of all however came from the front page of *The Wilmington Journal* in North Carolina on August 13th:

How they Murder in Massachusetts.

The implication was that the information in the article below that headline would be completely unfathomable to anyone outside of the Bay State. But almost as if to counter that charge, *The Worcester Daily Spy* two months later printed the following on October 11th:

> Had such a crime been committed in any section of the country outside of the New England states, and such strong circumstantial evidence existed against an accused man as today exists against Samuel J. Frost, the murderer would have been launched into eternity on the nearest available tree by an infuriated mob; but, thanks to the law abiding citizens of this state, no such scene of violence was enacted.

Such was the Frost case that both newspapers were indeed correct, even though they seemingly ran counter to one another. North Carolina readers could take comfort knowing that *they didn't kill* like people in Massachusetts did. Meanwhile, readers in Massachusetts could take pride in the fact *they didn't lynch* like those crazy people in North Carolina surely would have!

That said, it should be noted that *The Spy's* point was almost rendered untrue on the night of Frost's arrest. As *The Boston Post* pointed out in its initial story on August 3rd:

> The suspicions which had been entertained against Frost were increased tenfold, and there was no longer any doubt in the minds of the townspeople that he was the murderer. There was even some talk of lynch law, but the better sentiment and calmer judgment of the law-abiding people prevailed.

In fact, it was Frost himself who had expressed relief when Sheriff Bothwell came to get him in the attic, as he had feared it was a member of the angry mob coming to lynch him. "Law abiding citizens" of Massachusetts may have prevailed, but there was in fact "an infuriated mob" on that farm the night of July 31st.

Frost was formally indicted for murder in Fitchburg Superior Court on August 12th. The legal significance of that appearance was that since the penalty for his crime could be death, Frost's case was immediately kicked up to the state's highest court, the Supreme Judicial Court of Massachusetts. But for much of the press, the significance was this was their first chance to actually lay their eyes on the accused. As The August 19th *Worcester West Chronicle* noted, both "the court and railway stations were crowded to see him, many coming several miles." Samuel J. Frost had become a sensation, and people wanted to catch a glimpse of the notorious alleged murderer. But if *The Worcester West Chronicle* is to be believed, those who did get a look at Samuel were surely taken aback. *The Chronicle* was the first paper to print a physical description of him, and it wasn't pretty:

> He had a weakly, cadaverous look, with ragged brown clothes, and a repulsive, tramp-like appearance generally. He was gloomy most of the time, and when he does laugh he unsheathes a massive set of dirty teeth.

Remember, this was the "cleaned up" Frost. The first thing Sheriff
Bothwell did with Samuel upon arriving at the Barre Jail was to give
him a bath, and Carrie had brought a clean set of clothes for him that
morning, per Bothwell's request. So its readers could only wonder how
The Chronicle would have described the "not so cleaned up" Frost who
rode with Bothwell to Barre the night of his arrest.

The *Athol Transcript* also noted Frost's Fitchburg hearing. It
offered an otherwise insignificant two-sentence report, except that the
paper referred to Frost in an unusual way:

> Frost, the Petersham butcher, has been formally indicted for
> murder in the first degree. And yet he says he didn't.

This would be the only time the phrase "the Petersham butcher" would
appear in print. For some reason the macabre moniker did not stick
to Samuel, and he would almost uniformly be referred to as "the Petersham Murderer" going forward. Even *The Transcript* editors opted
against using the term ever again.

The Transcript did have a juicy tidbit two weeks later however,
which contained a number of descriptive phrases for Samuel. But more
importantly, the item gave a tiny glimpse into what Carrie Frost was
dealing with at the time:

> Frost, the murderer, milk spiller, mutilator, and practical sexton
> and resurrectionist, has written his wife requesting her to come
> and see him, and bring the children, some huckleberries, and
> some clean clothes. She failed to respond.

It had been less than a month since his arrest, and yet here was Samuel
asking his wife to visit him, and to bring some treats! One can only
imagine what was going through Carrie's mind when she read that letter, especially the huckleberries request. While it was factually accurate
to say, "She failed to respond," that last line could only hint at what her
real reaction to Samuel's letter must have been.

Nine days after that item was published in *The Transcript*,
Frost appeared in front of the Massachusetts Supreme Judicial Court
in Worcester. He did not yet have legal representation, and he clearly
could not afford any. As a result, Justice Charles Devens, the man now
in charge of Frost's future, assigned the case to attorney John Hopkins
of Millbury. Devens also promised to appoint an additional attorney

at a future date to assist Hopkins. In the meantime, the formal indictment facing Frost was read in court, and it was printed in *The Worcester Daily Spy* the next day:

> The first count charged the killing with malice aforethought, with a hammer, by striking Towne on the head, by which blow he instantly died; second, with beating Towne on the head, breast, back and belly, and then casting him on the floor, by which means he came to his death; third, with killing Towne by means unknown; fourth, by killing Towne with a piece of iron which the grand jury were unable to describe. To that indictment the prisoner pleaded not guilty.

Following that item, the papers went silent on the case. Nary a word was printed about Samuel for nearly a month. The attorneys were busy prepping their cases, Frost had no new court appearances in that time, and his jailers in Worcester were providing no information about their infamous prisoner. Until something new happened, the papers had nothing to give their readers. *The Worcester Daily Spy* finally broke the silence on October 8th with this brief update:

> The Petersham murderer, Samuel J. Frost, was brought into court and formally notified of the appointment of John Hopkins Esq. of Millbury, and George H. Ball Esq. of this city, as his counsel at his trial, which is fixed for next Tuesday morning at ten o'clock. Frost signified his assent and was remanded to jail.

Just like that, interest in the case shot right back up. Frost's trial would begin the following week on October 12th, 1875, just barely three months after Towne's murder. Hopkins finally had his assistant, George Ball, and together the two men had a mere FIVE days to finish preparing for the most anticipated courtroom drama in Massachusetts all year. So while the newspapers had gone "Frost cold" for most of September, the trial of "the Petersham Butcher" was about to make the presses run hotter than hell in the middle of October.

Judge Charles Devens
(Photo courtesy of Wikipedia)

The Big Six

As advertised, *Commonwealth v. Samuel J. Frost* commenced at precisely ten o'clock on the morning of October 12th. The defendant was a small, insignificant man who was known to few prior to his arrest. The principal players who would help determine his fate however were men of great stature and accomplishment, and most of them were (or would become) household names throughout the Commonwealth.

The Judges

The law in Massachusetts in 1875 stated that any potential death penalty case had to be presided over by not one, but two justices of the Supreme Judicial Court. In Frost's case those two men were Justice Charles Devens and Justice James Colt.

Charles Devens Jr. was 55 years old in 1875. He was raised in Charlestown, Massachusetts and attended the prestigious Boston Latin School. He matriculated to Harvard College '38, and then graduated from Harvard Law School in 1840. After practicing law for nearly a decade, Devens was elected to the Massachusetts State Senate before serving as U.S. Marshal for Massachusetts at the behest of President Millard Fillmore. But it was in the Civil War where Devens cemented his reputation. In 1861 he was nearly killed when a bullet hit him in the chest as he urged retreating Union troops to hold their ground at the Battle of Balls Bluff. Seven months later (after having been promoted to Brigadier General) he was again wounded in the Battle of Seven Pines. He survived the Battle of Antietam unscathed, although his horse was shot out from under him during the action. Then came the Battle of Fredericksburg, where Devens truly became a legend. He was once again injured as Stonewall Jackson's men routed the Union soldiers, but despite the severity of his wound, Devens remounted and refused to leave the battle until all his men had been safely sheltered. As a result of that bravery, none other than General Ulysses S. Grant wrote to Secretary of War Edward Stanton in 1865 recommending that Devens be promoted to the rank of Major General. (Nothing came of the recommendation once the war ended however.) Following the war, Devens was assigned to serve on the Massachusetts Superior Court, and six years later he was appointed to the Massachusetts Supreme Judicial Court. And two years after Frost's trial, President Rutherford B. Hayes would ask Devens to serve as Attorney General for the United States, which he did from 1877-81. He was absolutely one of the Commonwealth's finest, so much so that the town of Devens, Massachusetts, would so be named in his honor.

While Devens brought cachet, the man primarily in charge of the trial was James D. Colt. He was raised in the far western part of Massachusetts in Pittsfield. Colt attended Williams College '38 and graduated from Harvard Law School in 1841, a year after Devens. While running his own law practice, Colt also served as a Selectman in Pittsfield and then as a member of the Massachusetts House of Representatives. Upon the creation of the Berkshire County Superior Court, Colt was asked to serve, but he wasn't yet ready to give up private practice and so he turned down the job. (The next year, 1860, Colt had as clients Lemuel Shaw and his son-in-law, one Herman Melville!) Colt then accepted a position on the Supreme Judicial Court in 1865, where he served for the next 16 years until his death.

The Prosecutors

There were two men who would be prosecuting Samuel J. Frost on behalf of the Commonwealth of Massachusetts. The first was the state's highest prosecutor, Attorney General Charles Russell Train. He grew up in Framingham, Massachusetts, attended Brown University '37, and Harvard Law '41. (Train, Devens, and Colt all attended Harvard Law together in 1840.) Train was first a State Representative and then a U.S. District Attorney for Massachusetts. Then in 1852 he actually *turned down* an appointment to the U.S. Supreme Court. He served as a United States Congressman from 1859-63, and during that time he was a member of the committee that expelled the confederate West H. Humphreys from Congress. He volunteered as an aide to General George Gordon in 1863 and served with him in the Battle of Antietam. Train returned to the Massachusetts Legislature and then became Attorney General for the Commonwealth in 1871, a post he would hold until 1878. He died in 1885, and amongst his pallbearers were four former Massachusetts Governors and a former United States Attorney General, one Charles Devens.

Joining Attorney General Train for the prosecution was the

Worcester County District Attorney, Hamilton Barclay Staples. Twelve years younger than Train, Staples was born on Valentine's Day, 1829, in Mendon, Massachusetts. He studied at the prestigious Worcester Academy and then attended Brown University '51, where he finished second in his class. After studying law under Rhode Island's future famous Chief Justice Samuel Ames, Staples returned to Mendon and established his own private practice. He became District Attorney for the "Middle District" (Worcester County) in 1873 and remained in that post until 1881, when he was appointed to the Massachusetts Superior Court. He served on the state's second highest court for ten years until his death in 1891.

So the bad news for Samuel J. Frost was that the Commonwealth had four of its most respected men handling his case. It was unlikely that much was going to get past Devens and Colt (should the need arise), and outmaneuvering Train and Staples was going to be extremely difficult. But the good news for Frost was that the two men Devens had appointed to defend him had excellent pedigrees as well.

The Defense Team

John Hopkins was the first attorney assigned to Frost's case. Born in England in 1840, his parents came to America when he was two. (His mother died on the voyage over.) He attended Phillips Andover Academy and then graduated from Dartmouth College in 1862. He opened his law practice in Millbury and later partnered with John R. Thayer, the future Congressman. Active in local politics, Hopkins served both as the Chairman of the Board of Selectmen and the Chairman of the School Committee in Millbury. He would later serve in the Massachusetts State Senate, where in 1883 he was notably the Chairman of the Special Committee on Women's Suffrage. The year prior he was also the Democratic candidate for Congress for the "Middle District." In 1891 Hopkins was appointed to the Massachusetts Superior Court, thereby making him the only man born in England to ever serve on the Superior Court. In a strange twist of fate, Hopkins served alongside Hamilton Barclay Staples on that court for several months in 1891, some 16 years after the two men opposed one another in the Samuel J. Frost case.

Joining Hopkins for the defense was George Homer Ball. By far the youngest of the six men involved in the case, he had just turned 27 at the time of the trial. Ball was born in Milford, Massachusetts and he attended Lawrence Academy before graduating from both Harvard '69

and Harvard Law '71. In another strange twist, it was none other than
Hamilton Barclay Staples who had urged Ball to go to college to study
law. After graduating, Ball actually worked for a time under Staples.
Stranger still, Ball left Staples to work for J. Henry Hill, who was once a
law partner of Charles Devens! (Hill incidentally was born and raised
in Petersham.) Following Frost's case, Ball would serve as Assistant
District Attorney for several years under Staples before being elected to
the Massachusetts House of Representatives. He was well on his way
to enjoying a distinguished legal and/or political career (he seemed
destined for a high judgeship) until his father-in-law died suddenly in
1882. As a result of the unexpected death, Ball left public service to
take over the family railroad business. It proved to be a wise decision,
as he would find his way onto the board of directors for several rail-
roads across the country, and as his obituary in 1904 stated, Ball died "a
man of great wealth."

Finding a more impressive group to gather in that courthouse
that Tuesday morning would have been nearly impossible. And assem-
bling a group that had less in common with the defendant would have
been equally difficult. Frost was an isolated and unknown struggling
farmer, whereas these six were all Ivy League educated men who had
each found tremendous professional success. Yet, while Frost knew
next to nothing about any of them, they each knew plenty about him.
They'd all done their homework, and they were ready to do battle over
the fate of the man who'd brought them all together in the first place.

But before the anticipated clash could begin, the young upstart
George Ball surprised everyone with a pre-trial request which sought
to make Massachusetts' legal history:

> (Ball) "May it please your Honors, the prisoner at the bar at this
> time desires to present a petition to your Honors for a change of
> venue for the trial of this cause."
> (Colt) "What is the statute to which you have reference?"
> (Ball) "The statute is that of 1871, chapter 240, section 1."

The 1871 statute Ball cited reads as follows:

> Upon the petition of a person indicted for a capital offence, the
> court may order a change of venue to any county adjoining the
> county in which the indictment was found, when in the opin-

ion of the court an impartial trial cannot be had in the county
where the case is pending; and on such order the court shall
have full jurisdiction in the premises in the county to which
such change be made. All other proceedings in such case shall
be the same, as nearly as may be, as if the indictment had been
originally entered in such adjoining county.

Having been completely caught off-guard by Ball's request, Colt
and Devens conferred quietly on the bench for several minutes. When
they were done, Colt explained that while the Court was aware of the
provision Ball was citing, no defendant in the Commonwealth had ever
tried to use the provision since the law had been enacted. As such,
the Court had no guiding principle in handling such a request. The
judge stated that he took the statute to mean that such a request should
have occurred long before the jury had been assembled, not at the very
moment the trial was to start. But Colt offered that the Court would
be willing to overlook that and issue a quick ruling on the matter if oral
arguments were not required. Attorney Hopkins would have none of
that however, and he loudly objected to Colt's suggestion:

> It is the desire of the prisoner that an argument be had upon
> this petition. It is true that the jurors are assembled, but I think
> the facts will show that the petition is filed as early as it could
> possibly be filed. The facts upon which we rely became obvious
> to the counsel yesterday, and it is the first opportunity we have
> had of presenting the petition of the prisoner for a change of
> venue.

Not happy but with little legal ground under him, Judge Colt turned to
the Attorney General for help on the matter. But Train just shook his
head and meekly said, "I have nothing to suggest." Colt gave Train a
glare, sighed, and then addressed the jury. "It will be necessary for you
to retire for a time to an adjourning room. You will go there and wait
in attendance until your presence shall be required in Court." Once
the jurors were escorted out, a disquieted Colt turned to Ball and after
another sigh, he announced, "Mr. Ball, you may read your petition."

Frost's defense team had taken the court by surprise, and as a
result they had been victorious in the first skirmish of the trial. Having
done so, they now had the chance to make even more legal history by
winning a first-of-its-kind change of venue ruling. And since Attorney

General Train had no idea that such a request was coming, he would have to scramble to counter them. The advantage was clearly with the defense. Emboldened by Colt's acquiescence, Ball began:

> Your petitioner believes, and has reason to believe, that an impartial trial cannot be had in this county where the cause is pending, because your petitioner says false, erroneous, and highly colored narrations of the facts, and premature publication of the evidence upon which the government relies, have been published, and circulated throughout said county, that unauthorized and untrue statements of your petitioner's defense have also been made and circulated widely, accompanied with comments calculated to materially prejudice your petitioner's cause.

He then introduced as evidence a copy of *The Worcester Daily Spy* of October 11th, 1875, which had three full columns on page 1 detailing the facts of the case. Ball stressed that the article contained the inflammatory line, "had such a crime been committed in any section of the country west of the New England states, the murderer would have been launched into eternity on the nearest available tree." (Had Ball had time to do more research, he surely would have included the front page of the August 4th *Daily Spy*, which stated, "there is little, if any, doubt that Frost committed the terrible deed.") The defense attorney argued that anyone who'd read those words the day before the trial would inherently be predisposed to think that Frost should be hanged.

Ball then yielded the floor to Hopkins, much to the chagrin of Justice Colt. Hopkins, who had a flair for the melodramatic, launched into a long, theatrical speech about what an injustice it would be were this trial NOT moved. Hopkins' over-the-top presentation boiled down to three main points. First, he argued that *The Daily Spy* was purposely attempting to rekindle a hatred for Frost in printing its article the day before the trial:

> We say that if that opinion prevailed at the time in Petersham, and in the county, that there was a strong feeling of the defendant's guilt there, then time might have softened the feeling that existed against this defendant if the newspapers had allowed it to do so, but we find that the opinion then prevailing prevails today, because on the eve of this trial we find these statements

here. Then further, if a newspaper is the reflex of public opinion, we say beyond that, that it creates public opinion, and we say with reference to this particular article, that it has made public opinion in this county necessarily, that is prejudicial to the rights of the prisoner at the bar.

Second, Hopkins pointed out that the jurors had all been summoned to Worcester by the 11th, and thus there was every reason to believe they would have read, or at least been made aware of the prejudicial article:

Knowing that it was the most important public duty they would ever perform of such a nature as this, we say that a jury summoned under such circumstances would naturally read, hear of, and think about, anything of a public nature that was expressed in this way. We claim that in all probability a large majority of the jurors assembled here have read and understood the statements that are here made, and they will form their opinions upon, or they will accept, the opinion that is promulgated by the writer of this article, and they will start from the very outset with the conviction that in Petersham, in July last, was committed "one of the most atrocious and diabolical crimes ever perpetrated in this state."

Third, Hopkins asserted that by its very nature, *The Worcester Daily Spy* lent credibility to anything appearing in its pages:

This is a paper that has celebrated its centennial, a paper that has some authority, its opinion has weight and authority in this community, recognized as the old standard paper of the county, and coming from such a paper as that, the opinions expressed carry greater weight, and the facts that are reported in it, or the statements reported in it, are sooner believed to be true and to be facts, than if they appeared in an obscure paper of recent origin.

After grandstanding for *over an hour*, much to the perturbed chagrin of Justice Colt, Hopkins concluded the defense's argument by proclaiming that *The Spy* on October 11th:

So far ignored the rights of the prisoner at the bar, as to broad-
cast these things which tend to create hostility and prejudice
and enmity against the prisoner to such an extent that they
may imperil his life; and we now invoke the aid of this Court to
shield us from the evil influences which we say this newspaper
either reflected or created in its recent issue.

The moment seemed to call for theatrics, and Hopkins had delivered.
"Shield us from the evil influences" indeed! He was most pleased with
himself when he finally sat down.

Exhausted by Hopkins' histrionics, Colt turned to the prosecution and asked for their argument against the motion. While Attorney
General Train hadn't prepared to argue on this matter in advance, he'd
been in many courtrooms before. He wasn't about to be flustered by
the spur-of-the-moment antics of the defense. Plus, Hopkins' lengthy
appeal had given him plenty of time to strategize. The theme of his
argument could best be summed up in one word: relax. He began:

For ninety years or thereabouts, during which we have lived under the Constitution, this Court had no power such as is found
in the statue to which your attention is called this morning, and
since the passage of that act by the Legislature, now five years,
no practice has grown up under it, and this is the first applica-
tion that I have ever known for a change of venue in a capital
trial.

His point was, if no one in nearly a century of trials in the state had
needed such a change of venue, why would *this defendant*? Was Frost's
case *so extraordinary* as to warrant such a move?

Train then employed a three-pronged approach to show that
this case was the furthest thing from 'extraordinary.' First, he down-
played the significance of *The Daily Spy* by pointing out that it was but
one of twenty or so newspapers in the area. As such, it was in no way
the conscience of Worcester County. Furthermore, the article that
appeared on October 11th wasn't at all unusual:

You see nothing which indicates any pressure, hostility, or vin-
dictiveness against this defendant. On the contrary, you see the
same courteous and respectful attention given to a solemn judicial proceeding which you see in every county town to which

your Honors go, and nothing more. You see the same amount of interest in a capital trial which you see wherever you go to hold a capital trial, and nothing more.

Second, Train suggested that a ruling in favor of the defendant would set a dangerous precedent for the Commonwealth:

> If upon the case made here a change of venue is to be ordered, all I have to say is that capital trials, in my judgment, will be very rare in this Commonwealth. It would be within the power of any defendant at any time, to procure an article to be published in a newspaper on the day before the trial, and then, upon publication, to ask for a change of venue. And I suppose, may it please your Honors, the Court ordered this change to Hampden County, as the motion is put, and the case goes there, and you go there, and some enterprising publisher, for a fee, on the morning before the trial is assigned, should publish the article in the *Spy* as the best epitome of the case, the same motion would be repeated, and upon the same grounds the Court would find that the defendant could not have an impartial trial.

Third, Train used his intimate knowledge of Massachusetts' crime to show that there was nothing particularly unique about either this case or this county:

> The atrocity of this crime has been paralleled more than once recently; no more atrocious than the crime for which Pemberton was executed last Friday… take the case of Castley in Dedham a year ago this coming December… take the case of Sturtevant a year ago last June (in Plymouth)… take the case of Allen, may it please your Honors, a case which has become one of the celebrated causes in criminal jurisprudence, there was no difficulty in giving him a fair trial in the county where the offence was committed.

Train's message to the Court was clear: Massachusetts had faced cases like this many times before, and none of those cases needed a change of venue. Did the Court really want to buck that system because of Samuel J. Frost? Train asked the Court to deny the motion. And as he sat down, he was just as pleased with himself as Hopkins had been.

In theory there was plenty to consider as Colt and Devens weighed the matter. In reality however, there was no chance they were going to shut down the proceedings before they even got started. As the trial transcript noted, "The Court then retired, and returned in a few moments." Colt delivered the Court's decision by first noting, "This is a recent statute, it has not yet received any authoritative judicial construction." As a result, he offered up his own:

> Upon such reflection as we have been able to give this statute, we are of the opinion that the purpose of it was to provide against a possible injustice that might be done to a prisoner occasioned by undue excitement connected with the homicide, growing out of questions which divide and affect large masses of people in a given county, such as might arise from political, or even religious dissensions and differences... Perhaps the statute goes further, and is intended to meet a case where there have been several trials, with disagreements of the jury or without disagreements, and which have occasioned in the county much discussion and divided parties in sentiment on one side or the other, such as to prevent a fair trial in the county where the offense was committed... But it seems to us that this case does not come within either category suggested, or any that can be thought of... Upon the whole, the Court is entirely of the opinion that this application must be overruled, and the motion denied.

Hopkins and Ball had ventured way outside the legal box with their motion, and in so doing they demonstrated that Frost's very life was in extremely capable hands. But Attorney General Train had steered the Court right back inside that legal box, and in so doing he showed that Frost's potential death was in equally capable hands. The motion had been an exciting and dramatic start to the trial, but in the end it had failed. It was a harbinger of things to come for Hopkins and Ball.

After handing down his decision, an irritated Justice Colt announced that the Court would have to recess for lunch. That meant the trial would begin in earnest at 2:30pm, some four hours later than Colt had wanted. Of course, knowing who the government's first witness was going to be, it was no wonder Hopkins and Ball had delayed things for as long as they could.

The statue of Charles Devens outside of the
Worcester County Courthouse.

CERTIFICATE OF MARRIAGE.

No. _____

1. Full Name of **GROOM,** _Sam'l J. Foss_

2. His place of Residence, _Haverhill_

3. Age, _37 years_

4. Occupation, _Carpenter_

5. Color,* _W_

6. Number of the Marriage, _1st_

7. Place of Birth, _Meredith, N.H._

8. Father's Name, _David W. Foss_

9. Mother's Name, _Emma M. Smith_

10. Full Name of **BRIDE,** _Carrie Pinger_

(Maiden Name, if a Widow,)

11. Her place of Residence, _Haverhill_

12. Age, _34_

13. Color,*, _W_

14. Number of the Marriage, _1st_

15. Place of Birth, _Tilbury, N.H._

16. Father's Name, _Job Pinger_

17. Mother's Name, _Sarah Ann Pinger_

The Intentions of Marriage by the parties above named were duly entered by me in Records of the _town_ of _Haverhill_ according to law, this _sixth_ day of _December_ A. D. 18_61_.

Wm B. Eaton Town Clerk.

The parties above named were joined at _West Newbury_ by me, this _tenth_ day of _December_ A. D. 18___

Attest,† _David Foster_

Parker S. Cox, M. G.

* (W.) White. (A.) African. (M.) Mixed White and African. If of other Races, specify what
† Stating Official Station and Residence.

[Be very particular to fill all Blanks.]

Samuel and Carrie's marriage certificate
(Photo courtesy of the West Newbury Town Clerk's Office)

8

<u>The Wife</u>

The courthouse was again full by 2:20pm, and at 2:30 sharp Devens and Colt were seated. The clerk read aloud the indictment of willful murder against the defendant, and then it was time for *Commonwealth v. Frost* to officially commence. Colt signaled for the prosecution to proceed with its opening statement, which meant that Hamilton Barclay Staples had the floor. With all of Worcester County following the trial, Staples was eager to show that as their District Attorney, he was indeed the right man to bring Samuel J. Frost to justice. He began thusly:

> It is my painful duty to tell you all the facts concerning a murder which was committed in the quiet country town of Petersham, early in the month of July. It was one of the most shocking affairs, which causes society to shudder and ask of itself — where and when can we be safe?

Staples then proceeded to chronicle the events of the case in painful detail: the events of the morning of the 4th, the Rathbone boys growing suspicious, the alleged trip to Worcester, the finding of the first grave, the moving of the body by oxen to a swampy second grave, and so on. Then he told the jury exactly what made this case so shocking, and he did so with a little lawyerly flair:

> What was done with the body after it was then taken from its second grave? We shall show that it was cut and hacked into pieces and distributed to the four ends of the earth. The birds of the air, God's own detectives, were there, and their plaintive cries told a story which will need your attention.

Until that moment the jury knew that they would be judging a murder case, but they had no idea that it was *that* kind of murder case. Upon hearing the words "cut and hacked into pieces," the jury suddenly un-

derstood why there was such a large crowd of people outside the courthouse clamoring to get inside. Meanwhile, Justice Colt surely rolled
his eyes when Staples mentioned "the birds, God's own detectives." The
judge had heard many an over-the-top line used in opening statements
in his day, but he'd never heard one quite like that.

The District Attorney finished with a declaration he'd used
many times before, but somehow it seemed more appropriate for this
case than any other he'd tried:

> It is the position of the government of this Commonwealth that
> this murder was a wicked, treacherous, and premeditated crime,
> whose parallel has not been seen in this peaceful, law-abiding
> county for many a year.

In all, the opening statement lasted for over *two hours*, which was an
hour and a half longer than the already perturbed Judge Colt desired.
On the other hand, the opening seemed to fly by for the jury, who were
listening intently to Staples' every word. Plus, considering that this was
a capital murder trial, brevity was not the order of the day.

Had *Commonwealth v. Frost* taken place in 21st century Massachusetts, attorney Hopkins would have given the defense's opening
statement immediately following the prosecution's remarks. But this
was 19th century Massachusetts and that was not the case then. In an
1875 courtroom, the defense's opening came after the prosecution had
rested its entire case. As a result, not only did Staples have the jury's
full attention, he was able to roll right from his opening to his first
witness without the defense being able to challenge anything he'd just
said. That transition began with Justice Colt posing the simplest of
questions:

> (Colt) "Are you ready to call your first witness?"
> (Staples) "Yes your Honors, the Commonwealth would like to
> call Mrs. Caroline Frost."

The mere mention of her name caused the packed courtroom to go
pin-drop silent. Samuel may have been attraction #1 in this trial, but
Carrie was definitely #1A. The crowd had longed to *see* him, but they
very much wanted to *hear* from her. After all, the man she'd vowed to
love forever was fighting to save his life, but her brother had already
lost his life at the hands of that very same man. So where did her true

allegiance lie? Was she going to protect or punish her husband? All eyes were fixed upon the 39-year-old "matronly appearing woman" who was "clad in deep mourning" as she approached the witness box. Many questions were about to be answered, and Massachusetts was finally going to hear what Carrie Frost had to say about her husband and his actions.

Samuel and Carrie Frost's life together had been atypical for the 1870s. They first met in 1865 while working in a shoe factory in Haverhill, MA — he was a shoe cutter and she a shoe stitcher. They were married the next year in West Newbury, MA on December 6th, 1866. After living with Frost's mother in Haverhill for four months, the newlyweds moved to Newmarket, NH in the spring of 1867. A year later in May of 1868 Frost took a job in LaCrosse, Wisconsin of all places, and Carrie joined him there two months later. But Wisconsin turned out not to be to their liking, and Carrie was back in Dover, NH with Frost's mother in January of '69. Samuel followed his wife back to New England five months later. At the end of '69 the couple gravitated to Worcester, MA, staying there for a year and a half before drifting to nearby Grafton, MA. They stayed in Grafton from the spring of '71 until the spring of '73, when the Frosts finally settled in at Petersham. Thus, in the six year span between their wedding and their last move, the Frosts had lived in *seven* different locations. Such a nomadic existence was highly unusual for 1870s New England, and complicating matters further was the fact that in the midst of those moves Carrie somehow birthed four children! Samuel had clearly asked a great deal of his wife since their wedding day, but Carrie had remained true to him and she seemed happy enough through it all. Then came the events of July 4th, 1875.

Once Carrie was officially sworn in, there was an important procedural matter that needed to be stated for the record before anything could proceed:

> (Staples) "I desire that Mrs. Frost may be informed that it is not obligatory upon her to testify, unless she chooses freely to do so."
> (Colt) "The law of the Commonwealth, madam, does not compel you to testify against your husband. Whether you will testify or not is therefore a matter for yourself to determine."

The reason for Colt's statement was that just five years prior, in 1870, the State Legislature passed a law stating in full:

> First: neither husband nor wife shall testify as to private conversations with each other.
> Second: neither husband nor wife shall be compelled to testify in the trial of an indictment, complaint, or other criminal proceeding against the other.

What Samuel J. Frost desperately needed at that moment was for his wife to take advantage of the second part of that law. After all, Carrie was the only person the prosecution had who could positively identify the decomposed remains of her brother, she was the only one who could state with certainty when her brother died, and she was the only one who could provide the material facts as to the whereabouts of her husband in the weeks following the murder. Had Carrie wanted Samuel back home with her and the children, she simply needed to invoke this privilege and decline to testify against Samuel. Instead, after Colt asked her if she was willing to testify, Carrie nodded and stated matter-of-factly, "I am." Nine years earlier Carrie had given a two-word answer that made Samuel the happiest man in the world – I do. This time however her two-word answer had the opposite effect. Samuel was now in a heap of trouble, and he and his attorneys knew it.

Staples began his questioning of Carrie Frost with the necessary background questions about her husband, her brother, and their farm. But then he got to the heart of the matter, steering Carrie to the morning of July 4th. First she stated that Frank walked by her bedroom early that morning wearing his usual blue flannel shirt with the sleeves rolled up. Next she mentioned that she heard Frank pick up his milk pails as he headed out of the house towards the barn, and her husband soon followed Frank in that direction. Finally, she said that after some time had passed, only her husband returned to the house. That then brought Staples to what would be the first of several devastating exchanges between the prosecutor and his star witness:

> (Staples) "What time was it that he came into the house?"
> (Carrie) "About 7:00."
> "Did he have anything with him?"
> "He had a pail, a milk pail."

"Was there any milk in it?"

"There was not."

"Do you know whether that was one of the pails Frank had taken?"

"It was."

"Was there anything on that pail that attracted your attention?"

"There was blood."

"Whereabouts was the blood?"

"On the outside."

"I will ask you whether you ever saw your brother Frank alive after he left the house that morning?"

"I never did."

Carrie was the only one who could connect the milk pail to Frank that morning, she was the only one who could tie the blood on that pail directly to Frank, and she was the only one who could give an approximate time of Frank's death. Without Carrie none of that would have been possible, and the prosecution would have had a gaping hole in its case. It remains a mystery as to why Samuel brought that empty milk pail into the house after he'd killed Frank that morning, but had Carrie not testified against him, that mistake wouldn't have mattered. Instead that pail became the first major blow to her husband's case.

Carrie was just getting started. Staples next asked her about the night of the 26th, when Samuel had been suspiciously out of the house until the early morning hours:

(Staples) "Did he go to bed after he came in to the house the last time?"

(Carrie) "I think he did. I did not see him in bed."

"Did you notice the next morning anything peculiar?"

"I did."

"What was it?"

"A strong odor from his clothes."

"What kind of an odor was it?"

"Like a dead body."

Staples let the answer hang in the air for added effect. He had first used Carrie to place Samuel at the scene of her brother's murder, and now he got her to put the stink of her brother's corpse all over him. The only thing he couldn't get Carrie to do was place the murder weapon in

Samuel's hand on the morning of the 4th. But he could get her to do the next best thing. He asked her about that favorite butcher knife, the one she always kept on the windowsill in her kitchen:

> (Staples) "When was it that you saw that knife last?"
> (Carrie) "Just before I retired for the night."
> "That was on the evening of the 26th?"
> "Yes sir."
> "Did you find the knife the next morning?"
> "I did not."

Whatever Samuel was doing outside on the night of the 26th, he apparently needed that butcher knife to do it. And whatever he'd been doing had resulted in that "like a dead body" stench being all over him. Since the jury already knew that Towne's body was found in sections, Staples had painted a very clear picture for the jury, all thanks to Carrie.

She wasn't done. Following the butcher knife discussion, Staples brought her back to the morning of the 4th to get as much clarity as he could about what had happened inside the barn that morning:

> (Staples) "I want to ask you whether you heard that Sunday morning that Frank went out, and after your husband went out, if you heard any noise or sound proceeding from the barn that morning?"
> (Carrie) "I did hear a sound, like pounding."
> "Did you hear any conversation?"
> "I did not."
> "Did you hear voices?"
> "I did not."

The exchange was important because no one yet knew what Frost's defense was going to be. The presumption was that Hopkins and Ball were going to claim some sort of self-defense. But if the killing had been done in self-defense, then surely Carrie would have heard conversation and/or arguing prior to blows being struck. Instead she'd heard nothing of the sort. And while Carrie could only speak indirectly as to what went on in the barn that morning, she could give a firsthand account of her husband's behavior once he returned to the house, and that too was damaging:

(Staples) "I want to ask you if your husband assisted you any that morning in fixing off to church?"
(Carrie) "He did."
"What did he do?"
"He dressed the children."
"Had he ever done that before?"
"He was not in the habit of assisting me."
"I asked you whether he had ever assisted you off before to church?"
"He did not."

Staples couldn't ask Carrie why she thought her husband had decided to help her that morning, but he needn't have anyway. Everyone in the courtroom could easily speculate as to why he had.

The DA then spent considerable time with Carrie discussing much of the physical evidence — the horse blankets, the reins, the sacks that held two-thirds of Towne's body, her sons' hatchets that were found in the field etc. Carrie was able to link each and every item directly to her husband. With that done, Staples could have finished there with Carrie. But he had a more dramatic ending in mind, which would lead to an almost unbelievable scene inside the courtroom. It began this way:

(Staples) "I must ask you in regards to the skull that is produced, whether that is the shape and form of the forehead of your brother?"
(Carrie) "It has."
"Off the head, the cranium?"
"It has."
"Will you be so kind as to state whether you recognize anything in the eye teeth, in the appearance of the eye teeth?"
"Yes sir. They shot over a little."

A little more than two weeks before to the trial, Sheriff Bothwell had returned to Petersham on September 26th to meet up with sexton Thomas Aldrich. Together the two men dug up Frank Towne's grave so that Bothwell could bring Frank's skull to the trial as evidence. Staples now held that very skull in his hands as he showed it to Carrie, and she positively identified it as being her brother's. All the while her husband, the man responsible for bashing in the side of that skull, sat a mere ten feet away. The scene was already surreal, but somehow Staples was about to make it even more astonishing:

> (Staples) "I wish to ask you what was the color of your brother's hair?"
> (Carrie) "Brown."
> "Will you look at that which I show you, and state whether that resembles your brother's hair in color and firmness?"
> "It does. I can't see the color quite so plain by lamp light."
> "Suppose you step down nearer the gas, so that you can see with some distinctness, on a matter of such importance."
> "I should say it was the color of my brother's hair."

Staples had been at it for several hours with Carrie, and as a result it had grown darker in the courtroom. He couldn't have scripted it any better. The lasting image the jury would have was that of Carrie leaning in to get a better look at her brother's partially smashed skull as the two heads were illuminated by the flickering gaslight. It was both revolting and mesmerizing at the same time, and it surely made the jury even more sympathetic to Carrie than they already were. It was a perfect ending to an outstanding performance by the District Attorney.

Hopkins and Ball sat shell-shocked at the defense table. The damage inflicted on their client by witness #1 had far exceeded their worst nightmares. As for Samuel, he sat in the prisoner's box silently stewing over what had just transpired. While he'd known that his wife was going to testify against him, he didn't know she was going to do so *like that*. In fact, post-trial Samuel would complain bitterly about what Carrie had done. He didn't mind so much that she'd testified, but he deeply resented that she'd done so in such devastating detail. He found it to be both unnecessary and unbecoming, and he would rail against her in the months following his trial.

The burden of cross-examining Carrie fell to John Hopkins, who was facing a three-fold problem. First, he had to somehow shake the credibility of a witness who had the facts on her side. Next, he had to be careful not to be too aggressive with her. After all, she had recently lost her brother, and the jury was obviously sympathetic towards her. If he came on too strong, he might well turn them further against his client. Third, in trying to cast doubt on just how solid her memory was, he had to make sure he didn't lead her down a path where she might offer up even more evidence against his client. His strategy was to pound away at Carrie on minor and generally insignificant facts, hoping that she might wear down and maybe start to discredit herself. Only then might he be able to put some doubt in the minds of the jury. In pursuing this strategy, Hopkins had to go painstakingly slow over *everything* with Carrie. As a result, his cross-examination took almost three times longer than Staples' direct. (Staples' questioning takes up some forty-two pages of the official trial transcript, while Hopkins' occupies one hundred and twenty-four pages.)

Unfortunately for Hopkins, his strategy had two big flaws inherent in it. First, the trial had been delayed at the outset due to his change of venue request, and that meant that the trial would have to be adjourned for the night halfway through his cross. Thus, whatever wearing down of Carrie he'd done would be lost with a good night's sleep. Then there was the second problem — Carrie had her story straight. She knew *everything* that had happened, and she had gone over it multiple times prior to the trial. She'd spoken of it at the Coroner's Inquest, she'd given a lengthy interview with *The Fitchburg Sentinel* about it, and she'd rehearsed it with Staples several times as well. Regardless, she also showed at the Coroner's Inquest that she was not a shrinking flower, and so it seemed unlikely that she would succumb to Hopkins' tactics in any way. While John Hopkins had been involved in many court cases by 1875, few if any found him in a tougher spot than the one he was in with Carrie Frost.

As he rose from his chair, Hopkins skipped any pleasantries with the witness and instead started right in:

(Hopkins) "What time on that Sabbath morning did Mr. Frost come into the house?
(Carrie) "I think about seven. I don't know the precise time."
"Did you examine the clock to see?"
"I don't know as I did."
"Was breakfast ready?"
"No sir, it was not ready when he came in from milking."
"And that was about seven o'clock?"
"I think it was."
"And you had been up from about five 'till seven and breakfast was not ready?"
"Yes sir."
"How long before you had breakfast ready after he came in the

first time?"

"I cannot tell you just how long."

"I wish you would give me your judgment as to the time."

"It was not very long."

"Was it half an hour?"

"Probably it was. I should think, perhaps more. I cannot say how long."

"Was it an hour?"

"I cannot say."

"Well, is it your judgment that it was an hour?"

"I think it was within an hour."

"And that means then that you do not intend to fix it?"

"No sir."

"So if your reckoning is right, it was somewhere near eight o'clock when he sat down to breakfast that morning?"

"I think it was."

It was all rather silly. Whether breakfast was ready at 7:30 or 8:00 made no difference, and Carrie's inability to fix in on the exact time meant nothing. Towne was dead, and Frost was inside the house with a pail that had blood on it. Those facts weren't going to change based on what time Carrie had breakfast ready. Hopkins must have felt that exact times were somehow relevant however, as he next pressed Carrie on when precisely she'd left for church on the morning of the 4th:

> (Hopkins) "Where did you attend church that morning?"
> (Carrie) "The Baptist Church in Petersham."
> "How far distant?"
> "Three miles."
> "Did the service begin at half past 10?"
> "Quarter to 11."
> "What time, if you please, did you start for Petersham?"
> "A little before 10."
> "At your usual hour of starting?"
> "Yes sir."
> "After half past 9 and before 10, was it?"
> "About 10."
> "So that you started as you usually started, so far as time was concerned?"
> "Rather earlier than usual."

"What is it?"

"A trifle earlier than usual."

"How much earlier?"

"10 or 15 minutes."

"How do you know?"

"I noticed at the time that it was a few minutes earlier than usual."

"A few minutes earlier than usual, how many?"

"About 10 or 15."

"If you noticed that, how did you notice that?"

"By looking at the clock."

"Perhaps you could tell us what time it was that you started?"

"Quarter to ten."

"It is five miles to the church?"

"Yes sir."

"Services began at quarter to 11?"

"Yes sir."

"Now are you willing to swear that until that morning you did not start for church until 10 o'clock precisely?"

"That was my usual time for starting."

"So you have said. Are you willing to swear that you have not started for church, prior to that morning, before 10 o'clock?"

"No sir, I never have."

"Didn't the time of your starting depend very much upon the condition of the farm work, and whether or not the men could get the team ready for you? Is that not true? Was the time varying?"

"It could a little."

"It could 10 or 15 minutes, did it not?"

"It might have been so."

Hopkins finally dropped the matter, having "proven" that Carrie might have left a little earlier or later than she'd originally testified. The exact time had no relation whatsoever to Towne's death, but Hopkins harped on it nonetheless.

Next Hopkins quibbled with Carrie over who had actually broken the hammer used in the murder — her husband or his one-time helper "Irish" Mike. The hammer had been broken in January of 1875, and "Irish" Mike was long gone from the Frost farm by the time of Towne's murder in July. It was yet another puzzling point to dwell

on, but Hopkins did. He then disputed Carrie's assertion that Samuel had not done any farming in April of 1875, as if somehow Carrie's
insinuation was besmirching the character of her husband. But Frost's
April farming had no relevance to what happened in the barn in July. If
Hopkins was trying to make a larger point with these seemingly insignificant facts, he was failing. Instead it seemed as if Hopkins felt like he
had to question Carrie for a certain amount of time, and this was the
only way he could meet that fictitious time requirement.

Finally Hopkins decided to hone in on a matter of importance,
but he quickly wished he hadn't. Remembering that Carrie had testified that she'd heard "a pounding" in the barn on the morning of the 4th,
he set about debunking that. Instead he would help Carrie make her
point much more clearly than she had with Staples:

(Hopkins) "You spoke about hearing a noise on that Sunday
morning, like a pounding. Did you?"
(Carrie) "Yes sir."
"Can you describe the noise you heard in any other way than
you did describe it?"
"No sir."
"How long continued was it?"
"Not very long."
"Was it 5, 10, 15, or 25 minutes?"
"No sir, not nearly as long."
"As long as what?"
"As long as twenty minutes."
"Was it as long as ten minutes?"
"I should think not."
"Five minutes?"
"I should think not."
"Three minutes?"
"I can't say."
"Was it a sharp sound?"
"It sounded like pounding with a hammer."
"Like it was hitting into the ground?"
"Yes sir."
"Was it constant while it lasted?"
"Yes sir."
"Was it like blows?"
"Yes sir."

"Did you hear the cattle stomping about the barn?"

"I don't remember that I did."

"Did you ever?"

"Yes sir."

"From what direction did the sound come?"

"It seemed to be in the stable. It seemed to be in the barn, the front part of the barn."

"There were no outcries?"

"No sir."

The exchange was disastrous for Hopkins. During his questioning Staples had only extracted from Carrie that she had heard a sound, "like a pounding." But when Hopkins pressed her on that detail, he unwittingly prompted Carrie to add emphasis to her story by stating "it sounded like pounding with a hammer." Even worse, Hopkins actually asked her "was it like blows?" Staples must have had all he could do to not scream with glee when Carrie responded, "yes sir." While it was true that Hopkins faced a difficult task in questioning Carrie, he was making it discernibly worse with such horrific mistakes. It was as if Carrie was wearing him down and not vice versa.

With facts not working for him, Hopkins next tried to fluster Carrie with scurrilous innuendo. His goal was to insinuate that Carrie's brother Frank was a violent person, which he attempted to do three different times during his cross. He first broached the subject right before court adjourned for the night on Day 1:

(Hopkins) "Now, up to that time, when you had been residing in Petersham, had you had trouble with your brother Frank?"

(Carrie) "No particular trouble."

"Did he strike you?"

"No sir."

"Throw you down?"

"No sir."

"Kick you?"

"No sir."

"During that same time, had you seen any trouble between Frank and your husband?"

"In words only."

"Frequently?"

"No, not frequently."

He'd planted a seed, and it gave the jury something to think about for the night. When Day 2 of the trial began the next morning, Hopkins picked right up where he'd left off:

> (Hopkins) "Did you see Frank on your return?" (from church on a Sunday in May of 1875.)
> (Carrie) "I did."
> "Sick was he?"
> "Yes sir."
> "Drunk was he?"
> "He was sick."
> "Was he drunk?"
> "I think he had been drinking."
> "Did you have trouble with him?"
> "I did not."

Hopkins didn't belabor the point, but he had at least introduced something negative about Frank, which in theory could have made Carrie a little uncomfortable in revealing it. He revisited the topic for the third time later that morning:

> (Hopkins) "I asked you yesterday about the first year that Frank worked in Petersham, and you said that he had no difficulty with you, and that he did not strike you or throw you down or kick you. Now I ask you about during this last year, a portion of which he was there. Did you have any trouble with him?"
> "No sir."
> "No angry conversations?"
> "No sir. "
> "No blows struck?"
> "No sir."

In repeatedly asking the questions, Hopkins intimated that he knew more than Carrie was telling. She had answered his accusatory questions without emotion, but the implication of the questions had raised doubts. Had Hopkins been able to produce witnesses later that could counter Carrie's claim on the matter, he'd have had something. But he never did. Instead, he'd been simply trying to shake Carrie by attacking her late brother's character. In that he was unsuccessful, mostly because Carrie knew it not to be true.

Carrie was not infallible however. Hopkins was able to score a big point when he questioned her on the whereabouts of her husband on the morning of the murder. The defense had presented the timeline that Carrie saw Frank walk by the north bedroom around 5:00am, and soon thereafter her husband arose from that bedroom and followed Frank to the barn. But Carrie had also made the claim that she and Samuel did not share a bed after the murder, and she would not waver on the point. As a result, Hopkins was finally able to box her in:

(Hopkins) "Did your husband go into the south chamber that night at all?"
(Carrie) "I don't remember that he did."
"Don't you remember that he didn't while you were there?"
"I think I do remember that."
"You think you do remember that he didn't?"
"Yes sir."
"From which room did you see Frank that morning?"
"From the north bedroom."
"And at that time, your husband was occupying your bed, was he not?"
"I am not positive."
"Were you in bed."
"I were."
"Do you mean to tell me, Mrs. Frost, that you don't remember whether or not Mr. Frost was in bed when Frank came down?"
"I don't remember."
"If you don't remember that, do you remember the fact of his rising from the bed?"
"I don't clearly remember that."
"Do you remember whether or not he was in the room?"
"No."
"Do you remember seeing him in that room that morning?"
"Of course I saw him there."
"With reference to Frank's passing through the dining room?"
"I am sure he was there before Frank passed through."
"Are you sure that he was there after Frank passed through?"
"I think he was, but I am not very sure."
"Before Frank passed through, what was his condition as to clothing when you saw him, was he dressed or undressed?"
"Are you speaking of Mr. Frost or Mr. Towne?"

"I am speaking of Mr. Frost, in your room, that Sunday morning."

"I don't remember whether I saw him in my room after he was
dressed or not."

"And you don't remember seeing him in the room that morning
in his night dress?"

"I have no distinct remembrance of him after he arose that
morning, before he left the room."

"Have you a distinct remembrance of the fact of his rising?"

"I know that he didn't remain in bed."

"Have you a distinct remembrance of the fact of his rising?"

"I don't seem to have."

The exchange was Hopkins' best. Carrie had been able to remember
with clarity the time her brother passed by her bedroom door that
morning, and she was able to describe specifically what he was wearing
from that one instant she saw him pass by, but she somehow couldn't
remember if her husband was in her bed at that same time. She wasn't
even sure when he came into the room, strangely. Hopkins must have
regretted not beginning his cross-examination with this argument, for
he might have been able to build on it had he done so.

Instead Hopkins ended with two final points, both of which
had to do with Carrie herself and not the facts of the case. First, Hopkins wanted to make clear to the jury that Mrs. Frost had been in no
way cooperative with her husband's defense team. As proof of that he
produced a letter Carrie had written to him prior to the trial. After
Judge Colt allowed the letter to be admitted into evidence, Hopkins
questioned Carrie about it:

> (Hopkins) "Do you recognize this letter?"
> (Carrie) "Yes sir."
> "That was addressed to your husband's counsel was it?"
> "Yes sir."
> "What is the date on that?"
> "September 19th."
> "That was on the Sabbath, September 19th, was it not?"
> "I don't remember."
> "Was it in reference to a letter from your husband's counsel
> written a week before?"
> "It was."

"Requesting an interview with you?"

"Yes sir."

"At Worcester or at Petersham?"

"At Worcester or at some other place."

"I will read this letter to you. It is dated 'Petersham, September 19'...

Sir, it would be very inconvenient, if not altogether impossible, for me to go to Worcester this coming week. Besides, it would be of no advantage to meet, as I have nothing to communicate."

(Hopkins) "Mrs. Frost, were you in Worcester the very next week?"

((Carrie) "I think I was."

"Don't you know that you were?"

"I went at some time. I did go to Worcester that week. I did not think of going when I wrote your letter."

"Didn't you go to Worcester the 21st of September?"

"I don't know what day I went."

"Did you go to the Probate Court and take out letters of administration on your brother's estate the coming week?"

"Yes sir."

"Now after the writing of that letter did you not refuse to talk with your husband's counsel at your house in Petersham?"

"I did."

The point was clearly made that Carrie was in no way interested in helping with her husband's defense. It was a calculated play by Hopkins. Most men in 1875 thought that a woman's first and foremost obligation was to remain loyal to her husband. Samuel had been counting on that, which was why her testimony stung him so badly. Hopkins hoped that the all-male jury would be at least somewhat bothered by Carrie's shunning of her husband in his time of need. If they were bothered, then they might be inclined to look less favorably on her otherwise damning testimony because she'd overstepped. To help drive the point home, Hopkins ended with something that neither Staples nor Carrie could have anticipated:

(Hopkins) "Mrs. Frost, is it a fact that you have said that you hoped your husband would be hung, and that you would do what you could to have it done?"

(Carrie) "I never said it, sir."

"I will call your attention to your passage down on the Barre
Stagecoach. Didn't you positively declare that you wanted your
husband hung, and that you would testify in order that it might
be done?"

"Yes sir."

"You do want him hung, do you not?"

(Justice Colt instructed Mrs. Frost not to answer.)

Hopkins remained silent as he returned to his chair at the defense
table. Like Staples before him, he had ended strong; he'd gotten Carrie
to admit to wanting to see Samuel hanged. That was a most unusual
admission for a wife in 1875. While it didn't change the validity of her
testimony necessarily, it certainly had the potential to lessen its impact
if the jury now thought less of her. It was a strong point, but Hopkins
would be unable to produce any witnesses from that stagecoach during
the rest of the trial that could back up Hopkins' assertion as to what
Carrie had said.

Staples' re-direct was brief and consisted of two main points.
He first tried to clarify what Carrie said on that stagecoach, but Carrie only offered that "there was nothing direct" and that she "had said
nothing in relation to testifying." Staples then asked her about the
implied violence of her brother:

(Staples) "There is one point I wish to call the attention of your
honors' to. It is a question I will now put to the witness. I think
there may be some misunderstanding as to what her testimony
was yesterday. I want to ask you if you said yesterday in cross
examination that your brother ever struck you?"
(Carrie) "I did not say so."

That was it for Staples, but Attorney General Train had one quick question for Carrie. He asked her to clarify that it was the Congregational
Church that she'd attended on Sunday the 4th, not the Baptist Church.
Carrie apologized and said that Train was correct. While legally insignificant, Train's question was a subtle way of reminding the jury that
Carrie was indeed a faithful church-goer, unlike her husband. So if
anyone on the jury felt that Carrie had forgotten her duty to her husband, she certainly hadn't forgotten her duty to God.

While no one knew what the jury thought of Carrie's performance, the newspapers were universal in their praise of her. *The Athol Transcript* of October 19th, 1875, offered this review:

> For hours she answered the questions and counter-questions of prosecution and defense in a calm, collected manner, never once becoming entangled. She stood the fire of questions put in a sharp, puzzling way, and what was noticeable throughout was her parrying of the questions in a manner which indicated, correctly or incorrectly, that her sympathy were not with the prisoner, her husband, but rather were in the interest of the murdered man, her brother.

The Worcester Daily Spy added, "Seldom does a witness give more prompt and intelligent answers to the interrogatories than Mrs. Frost." And *The Boston Post* noted, "The Attorney General was heard to remark that she was an excellent witness."

From the moment the trial date had been set, the public speculated about what the wife of the accused might say under oath. Carrie Frost did not disappoint. She had remained true to her brother and had defied her husband's wishes. She'd told everything she knew to the jury, and she hadn't wavered on the facts when she was cross-examined. She had been everything Staples and Train hoped she'd be. The defense would have but one way to counter Carrie, and that was with Samuel. But the court would have to wait to find out if he was up to the challenge, because Staples still had two dozen more witnesses to call, and they would only add to Samuel's problems.

Carrie's Probate Court filing for her brother's "estate,"
which includes her signature.
(Photos courtesy of the Petersham Historical Society)

The _final_ **Account of** _Mrs. Caroline P. Frost_

Administrat _rix_ of the estate _Frank P. Frost_ of

late of _Petersham_

in the County of Worcester, deceased:

Said Accountant charge h _er_ self with the several amounts received as
stated in Schedule A, herewith exhibited, - - - - - - $ 2 8.3 0

And ask to be allowed for sundry payments and charges as stated in Schedule B,
herewith exhibited, - - - - - - - - $ 7 8.30

Balance, - - - - - - - - $

Caroline P. Frost Adm _rix_

Schedule of Personal Estate.

		DOLS.	CTS.	DOLS.	CTS.
1	Horse	100	00		
1	Harness	10	00		
1	Lap Robe	2	00		
3	Cows	100	00		
2	Calves	16	00		
2	Doz Milk Pans	4	80		
1	Watch	20	00		
1	Trunk	1	00		
	Wearing Apparel	15	00	268	80

Mrs. Mary Cook
Original owner of the Frost farm
(Photo courtesy of the Petersham Historical Society)

9

The Motive

Carrie Frost had laid out everything of importance between July 4th and August 1st for the prosecution. Following her testimony, Staples systematically called the Rathbone boys, J.W. Upton, Sheriff Bothwell, Coroner Shattuck, and Pliny Babbitt to give their versions of the events as well. When they had finished, the prosecution had answered five of the six key questions in the case. The 'who" was Samuel, the "what" was murder, the "when" was on July 4th, the "where" was in the barn, and the "how" was with that jagged piece of iron. All that remained was the "why?" It was the key question in all murder cases, especially ones where the death penalty was in play. Why? Why would someone kill his best friend who just so happened to be his wife's brother? It was a question in need of an answer, and Staples had one: MONEY.

Carrie, Bothwell, and Babbitt had all testified that one of the items found in Towne's wallet after his "disappearance" was a $325 note that he held against Frost. With Towne dead, that note would obviously never have to be paid. But that debt was just the beginning of Frost's financial problems. Staples intended to show that Frost had a much larger, more pressing problem than Towne's note, and that was what led him to commit murder. To prove his theory, Staples wanted the jury to focus on three men in particular: John Page, Stephen Goddard, and Robert Whitehouse.

John Page was the sixth witness called by the prosecution, sandwiched in between John Rathbone and J.W. Upton. He lived just down the road from Frost in Hardwick, and he'd done business with Frost prior to the murder. Frost had leased his entire farm to Towne for the year 1875. After a couple of months with little to do, Samuel decided to lease a smaller tract of farmland for himself from his neighbor, John Page. Further, Frost had mortgaged all of his personal property with Page early in 1875 in the amount of $500, and that money had yet to be paid back. Staples pointed out those two arrangements to show Frost had more debts to pay than just Towne's, but those debts were actually of secondary interest to Staples. What made Page such an important witness was the business deal he made with Frost AFTER the murder, on July 8ᵗʰ. That was the day following Frost's "return" from Worcester after "buying Towne out". Staples zeroed in on that deal:

> (Staples) "Do you know Samuel J. Frost?"
> (Page) "I do."
> "Did you see him in early July last?"
> "Yes sir."
> "What day of July?"
> "The eighth day, I think."
> "Did you have on that day any business transaction with him?"
> "I did."
> "What was it?"
> "I lent him some money."
> "How much money did you lend him?"
> "One hundred and twenty five dollars."
> "What did you take for this loan, anything?"
> "I took a note and mortgage."
> "Have you got the note and mortgage with you?"
> "Yes sir. (He produces the note.) It is dated Hardwick, July 8, 1875. It states, 'For value received, I promise to pay John Page on order one hundred and twenty-five dollars, on demand, with twelve percent interest.' It is signed, 'S.J. Frost.' The mortgage was on three heifers, one cow, and one horse."

So the day after Frost "returned" from Worcester, he mortgaged Towne's livestock with Page for $125. And it turned out that Frost had offered an explanation to Page as to why he needed that money:

> (Staples) "Now Mr. Page, I want to ask you whether on this occasion when this transaction took place, Mr. Frost said anything in relation to Mr. Towne or his disappearance?"
> (Page) "He said he had bought him out, bought this property off him, and he wanted $125 to complete the trade with him. He told me that he went to Worcester the day before and settled with him, and he went to California, or started for there."
> "Well, did he tell you how he expected this money would reach Mr. Towne?"
> "He told me that he borrowed Towne's money. He got a man to assist him in Worcester, and this money was going to be sent to

replace it."
"Did he mention the man's name?"
"His name was Stone."
"Do you recollect what his first name was?"
"I do not."

Thus, Frost's story was that he planned on using Page's money to pay back "Mr. Stone", who had lent him the money to buy out Towne in that Worcester meeting. There was of course no "Mr. Stone" or any "Worcester meeting", but on July 8th Page had no reason to suspect Frost was lying to him.

The jury on the other hand, would have every reason to doubt Frost's story once Staples questioned his second key witness on motive, Stephen Goddard:

(Staples) "You live in Petersham?"
(Goddard) "I do sir."
"Did you have any relation to Mrs. Mary Cook in respect to her farm?"
"I acted as agent for her."
"In selling the farm to whom?"
"To Mr. Frost, or Mrs. Frost."
"There was a mortgage given?"
"Yes sir."
"And a note?"
"Yes sir."

So Goddard was the agent who'd originally sold the Cook farm to the Frosts back in December of 1872. But as with Page, there was a more recent transaction involving Goddard that Staples wanted the jury to focus on:

(Staples) "Now, was there any further payment made on this note in July last?"
(Goddard) "On the 8th of July, I think, there was. Well, there was the interest paid, which amounted to one hundred and twelve dollars, and the interest for seven months at six percent on that."
"Interest was compounded at six percent, it was at seven percent on the note?"

"Seven percent on the note."

"And then the arrears, the back interest was compounded at six percent?"

"It amounted to one hundred and twelve dollars."

"That interest had been overdue how long?"

"About seven months, would have been the 13th of July."

"It was due last December?"

"Yes sir."

"And the interest for 1874 was due last December and was not paid till July. Now was any of the principal, was the one hundred dollars annual installment, due for 1874, ever paid?"

"No sir."

"That is still due?"

"Yes sir."

"Who paid the one hundred and twelve dollars?"

"Samuel J. Frost."

"When did he make that payment?"

"On the 8th of July I think, on Thursday evening."

"Are you certain about that day?"

"Yes sir."

"Where did he make that payment?"

"He made it at my house."

"Describe the money he paid you."

"He gave me two fifty dollar bills and one twenty dollar bill on the Ware National Bank."

"Describe the money in respect to its appearance of age, or want of it."

"I noticed in particular this money was issued in 1865 and it never had been in circulation by its appearance. Never had been done up, perfectly straight bills, never been in circulation. I should not suppose, by the looks of it, it was not worn at all, new money."

"Two fifty dollar bills and one twenty dollar bill on the Ware National Bank?"

"Two fifties and one twenty."

Staples had laid it out perfectly. When John Page was on the stand prior to Goddard, the DA had asked him specifically about the $125 Page had given to Frost:

(Staples) "How much money did you give him?"
(Page) "One hundred and twenty five dollars."
"What was the money? Describe the money."
"Well, I don't know as I could describe it exactly. I received a
package of money that morning, and it was new bills, I believe
pretty much fifties, twenties, and tens, I should think."
"There could not have been many fifties, do you remember how
many?"
"I should think two or three."
"What bank was it on?"
"I should think the Ware bank."

Thus, on the day after Frost allegedly went to Worcester, he visited Page
and received $125 against Towne's stock. He then told Page the money
was to pay back "Mr. Stone." Instead Samuel visited Goddard that same
day and used Page's $125 to catch up on some of his financial affairs
with Mary Cook. And there could be no disputing that the money in
question had come from Page just hours earlier based on both of the
witness descriptions.

Then Staples caught a break. While cross-examining Goddard,
Frost's own attorney John Hopkins made another blunder:

(Hopkins) "Mr. Goddard, have you as agent of Mrs. Cook, tak-
en possession of this farm, for the purpose of foreclosure?"
(Goddard) "She took possession, I did not."
"When?"
"The 13th of May."
"The 13th of last May?"
"The 13th of last May."

It was a question Staples should have asked Goddard but didn't. Inexplicably Hopkins did, presumably because he thought the answer
would be that Mrs. Cook had NOT begun to foreclose. Instead, Goddard said that she had. Thus, Staples could now show that Frost owed
Page $500 for his personal possessions, he owed Towne $325, and he
was in arrears with Mrs. Cook on the farm to the point that she had
begun to foreclose on the Frosts.

That then was Staples' answer to the question "why?" Bills were
piling up fast on Samuel J. Frost, and he needed to make them go away.
Staples posited that the only way Samuel could do so was to make

Towne "go away." That would buy him some time, as he could mortgage Towne's livestock to hold off Mrs. Cook. He could then harvest
his rented farm and Towne's farm, which he theoretically "bought back"
from Towne. If the harvesting of the two farms went well, he could
then pay off more of his debts.

There was a third part to Staples' theory on motive, and it
painted an even more sinister picture of Samuel J. Frost. The DA next
set out to show that Frost had been thinking about Towne's murder
long before the morning of July 4th. To that end, he wanted to bring the
jury's attention to one Robert Whitehouse. He first referenced Whitehouse in his opening statement:

> "As early as May 7th he (Frost) had endeavored to enter into an
> arrangement with Robert P. Whitehouse to join the Page farm
> and the Cook farm together and run them as one, using the
> same tools and harvesting the crops together. By this arrange-
> ment, we intend to show that the crime, which was afterwards
> committed, was contemplated as early as May 7th."

This was a critical point for the prosecution. Despite all of the physical
evidence and testimony against Frost, the defense could still make a
reasonable claim of manslaughter. In order to prove murder, the prosecution needed to show premeditation. Whitehouse was to be the link.
The problem for Staples was, he didn't have Whitehouse. He'd agreed
to be a witness for the defense. Thus, Staples had to present his theory
(at least initially) without the help of the two men who knew the facts
of any such "arrangement" — Frost and Whitehouse. His strategy was
to mention Whitehouse's name as often as possible, starting with that
opening statement. The name then came up again when Carrie was in
the witness box:

> (Staples) "Now do you know anything about a man from New
> Hampshire, Mr. Whitehouse?"
> (Carrie) "Yes sir."
> "When was Mr. Whitehouse down?"
> "In May I think."
> "Do you know of any arrangement being made between your
> husband and him?"
> (Hopkins) "This question it seems to me is liable to objection.
> She may know of her own knowledge, or she may know by

information from her husband."

(Staples) "State not by information from your husband, but by what you know yourself."

(Carrie) "I know myself that he was there. I don't know of myself that there was any contract between them."

"Did you hear anything said between Mr. Whitehouse and your husband, in regards to this other farm?"

"I think not."

"How long did Mr. Whitehouse stay there?"

"A few days. I don't remember the exact time."

"Do you know anything in regard to his coming again?"

"He was to come again and buy the Page place. He told me…"

(Hopkins) "Objection!"

Carrie could not testify about direct conversations she had with her husband (per that 1870 law), so Hopkins rightly objected and Staples dropped the point. But he had planted the seed that Frost and Whitehouse had made a suspicious "arrangement".

Next, while questioning John Rathbone, the prosecution's third witness, Staples referenced Whitehouse again:

(Staples) "And do you know anything about Mr. Frost taking the next farm below him- when he took possession of it?"

(Rathbone) "No, I do not know when he took possession of it."

"Do you know of his doing work there?"

"Yes sir."

"What do you know of his doing?"

"Well, he carried on the place."

"When do you think he began to carry it on?"

"I could not tell you."

"Do you recollect when Mr. Whitehouse was down?"

"Not exactly, I believe he was down some time in March."

"You remember that he was down?"

"Yes sir."

"Then, passing over exactly the time when, you say you do not remember that, do you know anything about any arrangement between Whitehouse and Frost in regard to the two farms?"

"No sir."

"Hear any bargain between them?"

"No sir."

Rathbone had virtually nothing to contribute on the subject of White-house, except that he vaguely knew of Whitehouse having visited the farm in March. But that was enough to allow Staples to remind the jury yet again about the suspicious Whitehouse.

That then brought Staples to his fifth witness, the aforementioned John Page. After he discussed his business dealings with Frost and the origins of the money he'd lent Samuel on July 8th, Page testified about an interaction he'd had with Whitehouse:

> (Staples) "Did Mr. Frost ever say anything to you about his being pressed for money?"
> (Page) "Well, he did."
> "When was that?"
> "Well, I should think – I don't know but he might have said something of that kind to me at the time I lent him the money."
> "What did he say?"
> "He said he was not going to be so bothered with having to borrow money, he was going to sell out to a man by the name of Whitehouse I think, or something. He was going to buy in with him somehow."
> "He said he was going to sell out to Whitehouse, or Whitehouse was going to buy in with him?"
> "Yes sir."
> "Did he have any talk with you in reference to your farm, the Carter place?"
> "This Mr. Whitehouse and Mr. Frost came one day to my place, I should think sometime in May, to see about buying the place."
> "Was anything definitively concluded?"
> "Nothing, only they came to my place and Mr. Whitehouse said he would let me know in a few days, within three or four or five days."
> "Did you hear from him?"
> "I have not."
> "Was anything said at that time about putting the two farms together, or running them together?"
> "I don't think there was."
> "Was anything further said at that time in reference to uniting the two farms?"
> "Not that I remember."

The key line in Page's testimony here was, "he said he was not going to be so bothered with having to borrow money." That meant two things: one, Frost was indeed bothered by his money woes, and two, he thought he'd found a way out of those woes. Staples wanted the jury to believe that the way out was by killing Towne and partnering with Whitehouse.

This was Staples at his best. After all, the three witnesses had little direct knowledge of the deal Staples was trying to prove. In fact, they all testified as to being unaware of said "arrangement." Carrie actually testified, "I don't know of any contract between them." Rathbone responded "No sir," when asked, "Hear any bargain between them?" And when Staples queried Page about an "arrangement", Page stated that, "I don't think there was." Yet it was through those denials that Staples had hoped to convince the jury that there WAS such an arrangement. (It was similar to what Hopkins had tried to do when he repeatedly implied that Towne had been abusive.) Further, in his opening Staples put a date on the "arrangement" — May 7th, which just so happened to be the week before Mary Cook began to foreclose on the farm. It all added up to one thing — premeditated murder.

But Staples' "arrangement" theory came with high risk. After all, the defense was soon to present its side of the story, and Mr. Whitehouse was scheduled to be its very first witness. There was every reason to believe that he was going to tell a very different story than the one Staples had offered. And if Whitehouse proved credible, then his testimony would go a long way towards disproving premeditation. Remember, Staples didn't just *suggest* that there was an "arrangement," he'd stated it *definitively* as fact. Only Mr. Whitehouse could know that for sure, and it was time for the court to hear from the man himself.

District Attorney Hamilton Barclay Staples
(As printed in the book *The Worcester of Eighteen Hundred and Ninety-Eight*)

10

The Mystery Man

When the prosecution finally rested its case after producing some thirty witnesses, George Homer Ball rose to give the opening statement for the defense. Unlike Staples, who had talked for over two hours during his opening statement, Ball took less than thirty minutes to deliver his. His message was simple and straightforward:

> We come here to present testimony which shall show to you that the prisoner is not guilty of the crime which is claimed in the indictment. We shall admit that he killed his brother-in-law, that the blood of his fellow man is on his hands, but we shall show that he did it not in malice… There was no malice about it, no planning, but when the blow was struck it was done during a struggle between the two men. We shall account for all the little incidents which the government have introduced as evidence, and we expect to prove to you that the prisoner is not guilty of murder with malice.

Frost had killed Towne, Ball conceded the point. But he intended to show that Frost hadn't done so premeditatedly; rather, he had killed Towne during an impromptu struggle between the two men. Hence, the defense felt this was a case of manslaughter, not murder, which would eliminate the possibility of the death penalty for their client.

There were three main objectives to the defense strategy. First, Ball reminded the jury:

> "What is done to the body after death does not enter into the commission of the crime."

Ball couldn't say this loudly enough. The butchering of Towne's corpse was of course the most shocking aspect of the case, and it inherently prejudiced most people's view of Frost. Ball had to drive home the point that in the eyes of the law that fact was irrelevant. Frost was on

trial for what he had down to 'alive' Frank, not to 'dead' Frank. It was
one thing for the general public to fixate on that aspect of the case, but
it was not for the jury to do so. However, the problem Ball had in making the point was that the louder he said it, the more he reminded the
jury about the very thing he wanted them to forget — that Frost had
hacked up Towne's corpse.

Ball's second goal was to discredit Staples' theory on motive:

> "We shall show you that Mr. Frost had no motive to commit
> murder, that he was not short of money, or that he coveted the
> property of Mr. Towne."

If the defense team could prove this, then they would be much closer
to getting the desired manslaughter conviction. If they could show that
Frost wasn't burdened by money woes, then much of the prosecution's
case would crumble. This was a big IF however.

Third, the defense had to chip away at premeditation. This was
vital in staving off the death penalty for their client. As such, Ball was
acutely aware that he had to counter the inference made by Staples of
a nefarious deal struck between Frost and the mysterious Mr. Whitehouse. Thus, while Ball did not mention Carrie Frost, John Rathbone,
J.W. Upton, or any other witness directly by name in his opening, he
did do so in reference to Frost's alleged business partner:

> We shall show you that when Mr. Frost contemplated the
> buying of a farm in connection with Mr. Whitehouse, it was in
> contemplation that Towne should leave the place. There was no
> malice about it.

That then was the defense plan: the butchery was irrelevant,
Frost was not in need of money, and there was no sinister plot in place.
If Ball could back up those pronouncements, Frost was looking at a
couple of years in prison at the most. The success of the strategy very
much hinged on what the real story was with that mysterious business
partner. Thus the courtroom was filled with both people and anticipation when Ball called defense witness #1 — Robert P. Whitehouse:

> (Ball) "Where do you live?"
> (Whitehouse) "I live in Middletown, New Hampshire."
> "Were you acquainted with Samuel J. Frost, the defendant?"

"Yes sir."

"How long have you known him?"

"I have known him from a child."

"Is he a native of your town?"

"A native of my town."

So that's who he was — a longtime family friend who lived in Frost's hometown. He was 61 years old at the time of the trial, making him twenty years older than Frost. He was likely a friend of Frost's father originally, and although he wasn't a blood-relative, Frost probably thought of him like an uncle. With that out of the way, Ball got right to the heart of the matter:

> (Ball) "At any time during the present year have you had negotiations with Mr. Frost?"
>
> (Whitehouse) "Yes sir."
>
> "When?"
>
> "Last May."
>
> "What time in the month, do you remember?"
>
> "I think it was about the 27th of May."
>
> "Where did those negotiations take place?"
>
> "I think to my house."
>
> "With Mr. Frost in person?"
>
> "Yes sir."
>
> "Will you state what the negotiation was?"
>
> "Mr. Frost came there to my house, and wanted me to come out and see his farm."
>
> "At Petersham?"
>
> "At Petersham, yes sir."
>
> "And what was the trade, what was the bargain between you, if there was any?"
>
> "Well, he came there to my house and wanted me to come out. I told him I could not come at that time very well, and he insisted upon me to go, and finally he stopped. He went to his family's house for the night, and he said he would be back the next morning after rise, and wanted me to go out with him very much. Well, he came back the next morning, and he didn't seem to go away without me, and I finally concluded to go with him."

Ball and Whitehouse had certainly rehearsed his testimony long before this moment, and yet *this* was not how it was supposed to come out. Ball had intended to show that two old friends were just casually discussing a partnership. Instead, Whitehouse was portraying Frost as being insistent bordering on desperate. The only response Whitehouse needed to give Ball was "we decided that I would head to Petersham to take a look." But for some unknown reason Whitehouse added the "he didn't seem to go away without me" part, which certainly implied that Frost was up to *something*. It was a troublesome turn for the shocked Ball, but he pressed on:

> (Ball) "You went with him to Petersham?"
> (Whitehouse) "I went with him to Petersham."
> "Well, what proposition was made to you at Petersham?"
> "After I got there to Petersham, he wanted me to go round and look at his farm, and also Mr. Page's farm, and I went."
> "What arrangement, if any, was made between you two?"
> "All the arrangement that was made was, I got there on a Friday night, I came away on a Monday morning. I told him I liked his farm very well, and I didn't know but that I would buy one half of it, and he told me what I might have it for, and I told him when I left, that I would go home, and if I could raise the money without sacrificing too much, I would come back the next Monday again."
> "Did you do so?"
> "I did not."
> "What did you do, if anything?"
> "Not anything. I was to write to him. I told him I would either come or write."

Whitehouse was doing a good job of showing that HE was not up to anything nefarious, but the same could not be said of his friend who was the one actually on trial. After all, Whitehouse had just admitted that Frost was offering to sell him half of a farm that had already been leased to Towne for that year.

Then things went WAY off the rails for the defense. Whitehouse testified that he did indeed write Frost a letter, which Ball attempted to introduce into evidence. This was Ball's big play, as presumably the letter would spell out "exactly" what the not-so-nefarious "arrangement" was to be. But then AG Train objected:

(Train) "Wait a moment. We will have the letter, I guess."
(Ball) "Very well." (Ball produces the letter.)
(Train) "Is that your letter Mr. Whitehouse?"
"(Whitehouse) "Yes sir."
"Is that the envelope it came in?"
"Yes sir."
(Ball) "It is postmarked August 21st."
(Staples) "Is not that long after the arrest?"
(Train) "It is in reply to some letter which he had from the defendant, and not a letter written as an apology for not returning on Monday morning. Now I would like to see the letter to which this was a reply."
(Train to Whitehouse) "Have you the letter which this was a reply?"
(Whitehouse) "No, I have not."
"Where is that letter?"
"It is at my home, I guess."
"Was that from Mr. Frost?"
"I don't recollect receiving any letter from Mr. Frost."
(Ball) "I offer this letter your Honors."
(Justice Colt) "Is that the letter about which he testifies? I understand him to say that when he went home he was to come back on Monday, and he did not."
(Train) "Is this the only letter, Mr. Whitehouse?"
(Whitehouse) "It is the only letter I ever wrote to him, after I went home."
(Staples) "Then it does not meet at all the question."
(Colt) "Upon what ground do you offer it, Mr. Ball?"
(Ball) "I offer it to show the transaction between the parties."
(Train) "Please let me look at it once more. (He examines it.) This is a correspondence between these parties after Frost is in jail, and this letter is mailed to Frost, addressed to the care of Sheriff Sprague."
(Colt) "Do you press it?"
(Ball) "I offer it."
(Train) "It is in reply to a letter which he had received from Frost, as your Honor will see, which he now denies having received."

Clearly Frost had written to his friend AFTER he had been arrested, and Whitehouse had written back full-well knowing that his friend was in trouble. Ball had attempted a sneaky bait-and-switch to get that letter introduced, and he had hoped that Train and Staples would not catch it. Unfortunately for him, AG Train did. The only question now was, would Justices Colt and Devens allow the letter anyway, considering it was the sole correspondence between the two men that spoke to the "arrangement." Ball had his fingers crossed, but deep down he knew what was coming:

> (Colt) "It seems to the Court that this witness is called for the purpose of showing the pecuniary condition of the prisoner prior to the alleged homicide, and to show what the transactions between this witness and the prisoner were in regard to a proposed purchase of the farm, for the purpose of showing what were his pecuniary circumstances, or his expectations, at the time when the homicide was committed. The evidence was admitted of what took place between the witness and the prisoner prior to the alleged homicide, as bearing upon that question. We do not understand that the evidence is offered for any other purpose. Now it is proposed that in a letter which appears to be written, on the face of it, in reply to another letter which is not produced, and which was written after the prisoner was arrested for the offense with which he is charged. It seems to the Court that it is not competent evidence as affecting the motive."

Not surprisingly, Colt rejected the "evidence". Surprisingly, he didn't reprimand Ball for being so willfully deceitful to the Court in trying to admit a letter which was written nearly three months after its suggested date.

Thinking that things couldn't get any worse, Ball continued on with Whitehouse. It would prove to be an unwise decision:

> (Ball) "Whom did you see when you arrived there?"
> (Whitehouse) "I saw Mr. Frost and two young men that was there."
> "Do you know what their names were?"
> "Mr. Frank Towne, I think I saw him there."
> "You saw Mr. Frank Towne at that time?"

"Yes sir."

"While you were talking with Mr. Frost, did he tell you at any time that the farm was under a lease to Towne?"

"I can't say positively."

"What was said by Mr. Frost, if anything?"

"He said he would like to sell me one half of his farm."

"What did you say in reply?"

"I recollect when I came away I told him that if I could get the money without sacrificing too much, I would come back the next Monday. If not, I would write to him."

"How much money was that?"

"About three hundred dollars, I think, that he wanted at that time."

"Did you know, at that time, whether there was any part of that farm under a lease or not?"

"No sir, I did not."

"Did you see Mr. Towne after your first arrival?"

"No sir."

"Did you have any conversation with Towne about the farm?"

"No sir."

For some unknown reason Ball was asking Whitehouse these questions that were leading to answers damaging his client. The testimony again confirmed that Frost was being deceptive for monetary gain, which was not at all what Ball wanted to show. In fact, Ball had stated in his opening that Frost did not have financial concerns, but his witness now seemed to prove just the opposite. Had Whitehouse been on trial, this would have been an effective line of questions. But it was Frost sitting in the prisoner's box, and none of this was helping him.

Then Ball surprised everybody in the courtroom by stating that he had nothing further for his witness. Everyone was stunned. Ball needed Whitehouse to show that there was nothing suspicious about the alleged "arrangement", and he had not done so. Ball needed Whitehouse to show that Samuel wasn't worried about money, and he'd failed to do so. And Ball needed Whitehouse to shut down any thoughts the jury might have about premeditation. Again, Whitehouse hadn't delivered. Everything Carrie Frost had been as prosecution witness #1, Robert Whitehouse had been the opposite as defense witness #1.

Although he needn't have since Whitehouse had helped him enough already, Staples decided to cross-examine Whitehouse. The witness had no intention of cooperating with the prosecution however, so things quickly became farcical:

> (Staples) "Did you go to Mr. Page's with Mr. Frost with reference to buying the Page farm, or seeing what you could buy it for?"
>
> (Whitehouse) "I did not go down there to see what I could buy it for. Mr. Frost went on some business, I think, with Mr. Page about the farm."
>
> "Buying it?"
>
> "I don't know whether buying of it or hiring of it."
>
> "Do you say to the jury that you don't recollect anything about that subject being introduced when you and Mr. Frost went to see Mr. Page?"
>
> "Of me buying Mr. Page's farm?"
>
> "Your buying it or Frost's buying it, or both of you buying it?"
>
> "I don't recollect that there was anything said about me buying it."
>
> "Was there anything said about Frost buying it?"
>
> "I think Mr. Frost said that he had the use of it this year."
>
> "Well, was there anything said at this interview about Mr. Frost's buying it?"
>
> "I don't know but what there might be. I wouldn't swear to it."
>
> "Do you remember whether there was or not?"
>
> "I wouldn't swear."
>
> "What do you think?"
>
> "I say I can't swear."
>
> "That is all you say about it?"
>
> "I can't."
>
> "Can't what?"
>
> "I can't say there was, certainly, or wasn't."
>
> "Was there anything said between you and Mr. Frost in regard to putting the farms together, running them together, his farm and the Page farm?
>
> "No sir, not that I know of."
>
> "Not that you know of? Well, was there?"
>
> "I think not."
>
> "Will you swear there was not?"
>
> "I couldn't swear."
>
> "You won't swear?"

"No, I don't wish to swear to anything unless I am confident of it."

"Then you are not confident that there was not something said about running the two farms together?"

"I can't say there was or was not."

And that was how it went. Whitehouse was not going to give Staples an inch, and Staples did not mind making Whitehouse play the fool. Mercifully it lasted only a few minutes, ending in ludicrous fashion when Staples asked again about the infamous letter:

(Whitehouse) "I wrote after I didn't go back that Monday. I can't say exactly what time I wrote."
(Staples) "Well, what did you write?"
(Whitehouse) "I can't swear what I did write."

The letter was postmarked August 21st, so Whitehouse knew full well when he wrote it. Further, he had brought the letter himself to the courthouse, and yet he was now unwilling to testify as to his memory of its contents! It was all so preposterous. Whitehouse knew the truth of what had happened, but he had been absurdly evasive about it. There had to be a reason, which wasn't good for one Samuel J. Frost.

Hoping for better results, Ball called his second witness. Sewall Goddard was a fellow farmer from Petersham who Samuel asked in April of 1875 to come to Frost's farm for the purpose of appraising the value of Frost's possessions. His five minutes of testimony boiled down to this:

(Ball) "Now can you tell us Mr. Goddard, what articles you appraised, and what the price was?"
(Goddard) "Four steer, $215. Four cows, $150. One yearling, $14. One horse, $175. One sow and pigs, $50. Two shoats, $25. Twenty-nine fowls, $17.40. Lot of hay, $200. One mowing machine, $60. One wagon, $40. One plough, $14. One sled, $8. One harrow, $10.
(Ball) "Do you remember what the total amount was, what they all came to?"
(Goddard) "$978.40."

What Ball hoped to show, presumably, was that Frost had possessions that he could have turned into cash had he been in such financial straits. Therefore, he didn't need to kill Towne for money. But what Goddard really proved, again, was that Frost was indeed thinking about money and how he might get it in the spring of 1875. And Ball had conveniently left out *one little fact* when he questioned Goddard. That omission prompted Staples' *only* question to Goddard under cross-examination:

> (Staples) "In making that appraisal, carrying out the items and footing the items up, was there any account taken of the various mortgages that Mr. John Page had upon all this property?"
> (Goddard) "No sir. There was nothing said about that. I did not know about that personally."

Staples needed ask nothing further, as the damage inflicted by that one question was plenty. Just as Frost was trying to sell a farm to Whitehouse that he had already leased, he was also seeking to leverage property with Goddard that he'd already mortgaged. In both cases Frost was being completely deceitful about it. What was becoming increasingly obvious was that the defense hadn't been able to find any witnesses that could help their client. Thus, Ball had little choice but to produce witnesses that ran a high risk of burning them, and both Whitehouse and Goddard did just that.

His third witness had at least some strategic value. Mary Emma Wheeler was Samuel J. Frost's sister. Her testimony in its entirety took all of two minutes:

> (Ball) "Where is your residence?"
> (Wheeler) "Dover, NH."
> "Are you a relative of the prisoner?"
> "I am his sister."
> "Have you ever visited his family?"
> "I have."
> "Since they have been at Petersham?"
> "Yes sir."
> "Did you know Mr. Towne?"
> "I did."
> "When did you last visit at Petersham?"
> "1873."

"And did you see Mr. Towne?"

"I did."

"Did you have any conversations with him at that time, Mrs. Wheeler?"

"I spoke with him."

"How long were you there Mrs. Wheeler?"

"From Saturday, ten o'clock, until Tuesday morning at seven o'clock."

"Did you notice anything peculiar in the relations between Mr. Towne and your brother?"

"I did not."

Ball smiled and nodded at Mary Wheeler, and then he nodded to Staples to signify that he was done with the witness. Her actual testimony had been pointless, but Mary Wheeler wasn't placed in the witness box for what she would say. She had been called to the stand for one reason — to show that somebody actually loved the defendant. She was as close to a grieving widow as the defense had, and so Ball used her. She wasn't much, but she was substantially more valuable than Whitehouse and Goddard had been. For his part, Staples realized that there was no upside to questioning Mary Wheeler, and so he wisely waived any cross-examination of her.

The prosecution had called some thirty witnesses to help make its case. The defense had called *three*, and they'd been disastrous. In fact, two of the three had actually bolstered the prosecution's case. To put it mildly, things were not going well for the defense. But Ball had one more person to call to the stand, and defense witness #4 had the potential to change everything. The time had finally come for Samuel J. Frost to step down from the prisoner's box and step up into the witness box. It was time to find out if the man who had caused his brother-in-law's death could now somehow save his own life.

Artist sketch of Samuel J. Frost in the witness box.
(As printed in *The Athol Transcript* on May 30, 1876)

11

The Defendant

(Ball) Mr. Frost, when were you married?"
(Frost) "I was married the sixth day of December, 1866."
(Ball) "Where?"
(Frost) "Haverhill, Mass."
(Ball) "At that time were you acquainted, Mr. Frost, with Mr. Towne?"
(Frost) "I was sir."

So began the testimony of the man in the eye of the storm. And in that innocent opening exchange, the defendant absentmindedly offered up his first inaccuracy. While Frost and his bride did live in Haverhill at the time of their wedding, they were actually married in the neighboring town of West Newbury. Such trivial details were the least of anyone's concern at that moment however. Samuel J. Frost was to be the last witness for the defense, and it was time to see if he could counter the testimony of the first witness for the prosecution — the very woman he married in West Newbury back in 1866. After all, his fate primarily rested in the question of which one the jury was going to believe more, Mr. or Mrs. Samuel J. Frost. If they believed her, he was literally dead. If they believed him, he would likely serve a few years in jail for manslaughter.

He also now had the chance to explain "why?" That had been the biggest mystery from the very beginning of this case. Why would a man kill his brother-in-law, who by all accounts was also his best friend? DA Staples had offered his theory, but all of Massachusetts was waiting to hear what the killer himself had to say about that. There was no doubt inside the courtroom that had the trial ended right then, without Samuel testifying, he was going to hang. But he was about to testify, and if he could tell a credible story that answered the question of "why?", it might just be enough to save him from the gallows. The question was, did Samuel J. Frost have such a story.

As he took his place in the witness box, all eyes in the court-room were glued to him. What they saw was colorfully described in *The Boston Journal*:

> Frost is a small, light man. He has an angular face with stiff looking beard and moustache. His eyes are keen and hard look-ing and his face has that peculiar blanched appearance which faces seen in the prisoner's dock so often exhibit.

The *Athol Transcript* depicted him this way:

> He is of diminutive and slight build, and evidently of a nervous temperament. There is nothing prominent in the appearance nor unusual in the actions of the man, excepting, perhaps a pair of deeply set gray eyes, which glance about in a restless sort of way. His age is 42, but he scarcely looks it. This morning he was dressed in a set of rough mixed cloth, while a stone pin was prominent on his shirt bosom.

But perhaps it was the *Boston Post* that gave the most poignant descrip-tion of Frost. It used only one line, but in that sentence the paper cap-tured both the gravity of the moment and the toll the trial had already taken on the defendant:

> The prisoner did not look as well as he has on previous occasions.

While everything hinged on whether Samuel could satisfacto-rily answer the "why?" question, the jury had to wait almost a half an hour to find out. Defense Attorney Ball first made Frost painstakingly go over his relationship with Towne from the time they first met in 1865 until their relationship ended on that July 4th in 1875. But finally, after seemingly endless questions as to what the two men did together on July 3rd, Ball arrived at the only thing that mattered:

> (Ball) "When you got up in the morning, do you remember whether it was a pleasant or stormy morning?"
> (Frost) "It was a pleasant morning."

While the weather in Petersham on July 4th may have been pleasant,

what occurred that morning on Frost's farm was most assuredly UN-
pleasant. And to hear the man responsible for someone's death that
day actually say, "it was a pleasant morning" took some people in the
courtroom by surprise. But it was that ironic response which introduced Frost's highly anticipated version of the events of that "pleasant"
morning:

(Ball) "Well, after you went out of the house, where did you go
to?"
(Frost) "I went directly to the barn."
(Ball) "Now, will you narrate to the jury as particularly as you
can what happened from the time you went into that barn till
you came out?"
(Frost) "When I first went into the barn, I stepped up onto the
door, I said, 'How do you get along?' to Mr. Towne. I can't tell
what reply he made to me, whether he made me any or not, I
don't recollect."
(Ball) "Where was Mr. Towne?"
(Frost) "Mr. Towne was then milking what we call the red heifer."
(Ball) "How far down the barn?"
(Frost) "About half way down, where it was partitioned off."
(Ball) "Was the place where he was before you reached the
white-faced heifer or beyond it?"
(Frost) "Before we reached the white-faced heifer."
(Ball) "Would you have to pass him in going to the white-faced
heifer?"
(Frost) "I did sir. I stooped down, there was a couple of pails set
right at my right hand as I went into the door. One of them was
a 12-quart pail, the other was an 8-quart pail. The 12-quart pail
was full of milk that Mr. Towne had then milked. I picks up
the 8-quart pail, which was nothing in it, hadn't been used that
morning. I passed down where Mr. Towne was milking. He
kind of replied and says 'I shall have time enough to milk them
this morning.' Says he 'I had just as soon milk her as not.'"
(Ball) "Go on, Mr. Frost."
(Frost) "I takes up this box and steps along and sets down and
commenced milking the white-faced heifer; my style of milking, which is not like most men."
(Ball) "What is your style?"

(Frost) "I generally strip this way (illustrating), what you call stripping a cow, owing to my hand. I can't close my fingers up, so I was learned to milk that way, and have always followed it."

(Ball) "You say you cannot close that hand?"

(Frost) "Not up close enough to squeeze a cow's teat to milk."

(Ball) "What is the difficulty?"

(Frost) "Nothing, only a stiff joint there, that is all. The heifer's teats are small, rather. I commenced milking her, and I got her about half-milked, and Mr. Towne finished milking the red heifer. He steps along by the side of me, and he says 'I don't like your style of milking much.' Says I, 'the heifer does, likes it pretty well.' He reaches out with his left hand and takes hold of the pail, and puts his other hand on my shoulder, the right hand. I quit milking, takes hold of one side of the pail, and puts my right hand right down to take hold of the box, and puts my foot up to move that. He kind of pushed me over the box, and he and I both went over. My head struck up close to this lintel piece, and he held me down. I gave him a polite invitation to get off."

(Ball) "Now state what was said."

(Frost) "Well, the language that was used between us both, I don't care about repeating here."

(Ball) "Repeat it please Mr. Frost, whatever you said there."

(Frost) "I will use other words that will do just as well."

(Ball) "Repeat what was said there, please."

(Frost) "I told him to get off. He says, 'let go of the pail.' Says I, 'I won't,' and one word brought on another, so we began to swear. Knowing that there was a lot of sticks over into this crib..."

(Ball) "One moment. You said you commenced to swear. What was said?"

(Frost) "Said I, 'get off me damn quick."

(Ball) "What did he say?"

(Frost) "He said, 'not by a damn sight, not unless you let alone of the pail.' Says I, 'I shan't do that, not until I am obliged to.' I reached over my hand, knowing there was a lot of sticks in that crib, I put my hand over there. The first one I got hold of was four or five feet long, and I couldn't pull it out from under the cow's head. I let go of that stick and goes for another, and it happened to be what I call my little boy's bat stick. It laid there, and I pulled it up."

(Ball) "After you got the bat stick, what did you do with it?'

(Frost) "I brought my hand up so, and struck him down in the face. No quicker than I done that, I brought it up again, and hit him again. At that time, he lets go of the pail he had his hand hold of, and he goes for the stick. But before he got the stick, I brought my hand up and hit him in the head again."

(Ball) "At any of these times when you were there struggling in that way, and you were hitting him with this bat stick, whether or not there was any blood drawn?"

(Frost) "The first time I struck him, I drew blood."

(Ball) "Whereabouts did you hit him?"

(Frost) "Hit him right square in the face and mouth."

(Ball) "Do you know whether that blood came from his nose or mouth?"

(Frost) "I can't say whether it came out of his nose or mouth, or out of both. I know that blood came out as he laid his head over my hand. I had my hand on the pail, and there were some blood drops dropped on my hand, and a few drops dropped on the pail."

(Ball) "Did the struggle continue then?"

(Frost) "It did sir. He got hold of the stick and undertook to pull it away from me. I had hold of it with my left hand; I puts my other hand up and takes hold of it with it. He commenced pulling and I commenced pulling. I got up and we had a considerable tussle for a few minutes, and being a considerably heavier man than I was, although he wasn't quite so quick, and didn't understand handling himself quite so well, we had it there perhaps from three to five minutes, there on the barn floor. I finally got the man down..."

(Ball) "Do you mean on the barn floor or in the lintel, the tie up?"

(Frost) "In the lintel, right in between two cows. We finally came down side by side, or nearly side by side. He was a little laid lengthwise of the lintel, down that way, and I was this way (crosswise). I was on this side, next to the crib."

(Ball) "Well, what was done there?"

(Frost) "After we got there, I kind of got his head down, and he got his arm around my neck. I had my hand there, into what he had on his chin, like that (illustrating). I held his head down there, I tried to get hold of a post that was there, about twelve inches square, to pull myself over. He was on his knees and on his right elbow, he had the stick that he had got away from me in his right hand. I held his head down with those chin whiskers, and he had my head down with his left arm over my neck. I could not succeed in pulling him over and he could not succeed in turning me. I reached my hand up on the kicking girth to get hold of that and pull myself up and pull him over, and I happened to strike my hand on that piece of iron."

(Ball) "Where was that piece of iron?"

(Frost) "That piece of iron laid on that kicking girth. No quicker than I struck my hand on that, I struck him on the side of his head. It didn't seem to hurt him any, that is, its didn't seem to affect him."

(Ball) "What hand did you have that piece of iron in?"

(Frost) "In my right hand."

(Ball) "What part of his head did you strike?"

(Frost) "The first time I struck him was right across here (indicating the cheek bone on the right side of the face)."

(Ball) "Did you strike him more than once?"

(Frost) "I struck him twice."

(Ball) "Where did you strike the other time?"

(Frost) "The other time I struck him on the side of the head, right back of his ear somewheres."

(Ball) "What happened after you struck him?"

(Frost) "What happened? He sings out 'By gorry!'"

(Ball) "Did he say anything else?"

(Frost) "Not a word."

(Ball) "Well, after he said 'By gorry!' Mr. Frost, did you do anything more?"

(Frost) "Said I, 'you are satisfied now, are you?' Those are the words I used exactly."

(Ball) "What did you do then?"

(Frost) "I gets up. I had that iron in my hand, and I takes this little bat stick, I takes it and pulls it out of his hand, and when I was pulling it out of his hand he takes and lays his arm under his head, and he straightens out as straight as (indicates a flat surface with his hands), he lay with his head on the floor."

(Ball) "Then what did you do?"

(Frost) "I goes out and I set down in the barn door."

(Ball) "How long did you sit there?"

(Frost) "I might have sat there one minute and I might have sat three."

(Ball) "What was your next action?"

(Frost) "My next action was that I went back and took up this pail and finished milking this white-faced heifer."

(Ball) "At that time did you know that Mr. Towne was dead?"

(Frost) "I did not know that he was dead, not until after I had finished milking the heifer."

(Ball) "How did you discover it?"

(Frost) "After I had got through milking the heifer I said, 'come get up and milk the other cow.' He made no reply. I turned around on my box facing to him and sat there about a minute or it might have been longer. I don't think though it was any longer than that. I told him if he did not get up and milk the cow I should. I got up and took this old stool that was cramped over on this box, I took that and threw it down over the other side of Mr. Towne across the barn."

(Ball) "After you discovered that he was dead what did you do?"

(Frost) "The first that I discovered he was dead was after I threw that box or laid it down over there. I took my hand hold of his hand and held it on top of his head. There, like that (indicating), and pulled it off. I said, 'For God's sake, are you dead?' Those were the words I used. He made no reply."

(Ball) "Go on from that point."

(Frost) "From that I went to examine him. I takes and rolls him up one side a little and carts him up. I feels of him, puts my ear down upon his breast, but it could not find or see any signs or sounds of any life at all."

(Ball) "Then what did you do?"

(Frost) "Then what did I do? I did not know what to do. The cows were in the barn and one of them was not milked, so I took this pail that I had with a little milk in it setting on one side of me that I had finished from the white-faced cow. I sat down and commenced milking the starred heifer. I milked, it might be one quart and might be no more than a pint. I got up and took that milk and turned it into the pail along with the milk that he had milked before. I took those two pails of milk and carries them into the house."

That then was Frost's answer to the question "why?" He had killed Frank because *Towne had jumped him!* The two struggled, and because Frost knew how to handle himself a little better than Towne in such a situation, it was the bigger Towne who ended up dead, simple as that. Frost hadn't intended to kill him, he only meant to end the scuffle and get Towne off of him. He was as surprised as anyone that Towne was dead. Samuel had told his story well, he hadn't stumbled, and he hadn't contradicted himself at any point. And he seemingly remembered every last detail from the entire ordeal. But was it enough? Would the jury believe that Towne, a man who had never been physical with Frost in the ten years they'd known each other, suddenly and randomly scuffled with Samuel that morning just because Frost was milking a cow that Towne wanted to milk? If the jury found it plausible, then Frost was in business. If they didn't...

While Frost had given his answer to the key question, he was far from done in the witness box. In an odd strategic move, Ball next asked Frost to explain the three key crime scenes on the farm. This was peculiar because Ball had stated in his opening that, "what is done to the body after death does not enter into the commission of the crime." Yet now Ball wanted Frost to answer why there was blood inside the barn, why there was a makeshift grave down by the swamp (where Joseph Upton found the buttons and the hair), and why there was the second spot in the corn field that looked like it had been recently dug up. Ball began in the swamp:

(Ball) "Well now, did you know of any such brush being burned in the pasture that week?"
(Frost) "I did sir."
(Ball) "Whereabouts?"
(Frost) "Down in the west pasture."
(Ball) "Who was burning brush there?"
(Frost) "Frank P. Towne and one Mr. Josselyn."
(Ball) "George Josselyn?"
(Frost) "Yes sir."
(Ball) "Did you go down to that pasture where they were burning brush?"
(Frost) "I did sir."
(Ball) "When?"
(Frost) "This was in July, on Wednesday."

(Ball) "What did you go down there for?"

(Frost) "I went down there to assist the old dog in getting at a woodchuck."

(Ball) "How did you know the dog was down there?"

(Frost) "I heard his voice."

(Ball) "Did you find him down there at a woodchuck hole?"

(Frost) "I did sir."

(Ball) "Whereabouts was the hole?"

(Frost) "Down on the edge of the swamp."

(Ball) "What did you do to assist the dog?"

(Frost) "I turned over a few rocks."

(Ball) "Anything else?"

(Frost) "Nothing in particular."

(Ball) "I will ask you, was that the place that Mr. Upton, the Selectman, has described here?"

(Frost) "It was sir."

(Ball) "Do you know that the dog killed the woodchuck?"

(Frost) "I did sir."

The prosecution had put forth that the swamp site was where Frost had attempted to bury at least part of Towne's body some time after July 22nd. That was why, they argued, the earth was turned over there and both blood and hair was found at that location. Frost's contention was that on the Wednesday before Towne's death (actually June 30th, not "July" as Frost testified), *his dog had killed a woodchuck there* and that was the reason for the blood, hair, and overturned ground. Frost later stated that John Rathbone was with him that Wednesday at the scene, but Rathbone was never asked to corroborate the story. Incidentally, Frost's old dog had played a critical part in multiple aspects of this case. He had played a role in the murder — Frost used him to distract the girls while Frost was in the barn dealing with Towne's body; he had played an interesting part in the arrest — witnesses wanted to shoot him because of his incessant barking; and now the dog had become part of the trial — he was Frost's alibi for one of the crime scenes!

Next, Ball asked Samuel to explain another one of the areas that the prosecution claimed was a freshly dug grave. This was the spot that Upton and his men were sure had once held Towne's body:

(Ball) "Did you have a white-faced heifer?"

(Frost) "Yes sir."

(Ball) "Did that heifer drop a calf somewhere about that time?"
(Frost) "On the Friday."
(Ball) "On the Friday before the 4th?"
(Frost) "Yes sir."
(Ball) "Whereabouts?"
(Frost) "Down the edge of the pines."
(Ball) "Did anybody go down and look for it?"
(Frost) "I went down and Mr. Towne."
(Ball) "Did you find the heifer?"
(Frost) "We did sir."
(Ball) "What did you do then?"
(Frost) "Well, we sat down there about a half an hour, then we got up and came home and got our dinner."
(Ball) "Well, after you got your dinner, did anybody go for the heifer?"
(Frost) "Mr. Towne."
(Ball) "Bring it up?"
(Frost) "He did sir."
(Ball) "After the heifer was brought up, what if anything was done with the calf?"
(Frost) "Well, we tried to make it suck a little, but couldn't succeed so Mr. Towne took him and knocked him in the head."

Thus, according to Frost that second alleged gravesite was in actuality just a spot where the white-faced heifer had given birth to a calf. That explained both the blood and the disruption of the earth at that spot. Further, because the calf wouldn't suckle, the two men decided to kill the calf, and Towne was the one who did it. This story was actually corroborated by Carrie Frost, who had witnessed some of it from the house.

Finally, for some reason Ball wanted Samuel to explain why there was blood found in the barn. It seemed unnecessary, considering Frost had already acknowledged killing Towne there, but Ball felt he could counter the prosecution's theory of the murder in so doing:

(Ball) "Well now, you say this bull stood in the manger, past down below where the white-faced heifer was tied?"
(Frost) "I do sir."
(Ball) "Did you cause that bull to be castrated?"
(Frost) "I did sir."

(Ball) "When was that?"
(Frost) "That was done of a Saturday, after Mr. Towne made his disappearance."

When Frost used the phrase "after Mr. Towne made his disappearance," several people in the audience snickered.

(Ball) "Who was there at the time of that operation?"
(Frost) "Mr. Stone and Mr. Rathbone."
(Ball) "What was done with the parts removed?"
(Frost) "When we were taking them out, we took and tossed them over into this crib and lay them up, I think, on to this stanchion piece. That is where we put them."
(Ball) "Now were those bloody? Was there any blood flowed during that operation?"
(Frost) "It is not very often you can do such a thing as that with out blood."
(Ball) "Was there blood about that operation?"
(Frost) "Yes sir."
(Ball) "Did that blood drip?"
(Frost) "It did sir."
(Ball) "Do you know, of your own knowledge, of any other blood being about the crib except the blood which came from that source?"
(Frost) "I do not sir."
(Ball) "When did this operation take place in relation to the disappearance of Mr. Towne?"
(Frost) "In about two weeks."

So Frost accounted for the blood in the barn as belonging to the bull's testicles, while the prosecution maintained the blood was Towne's. It was a distinction without a difference, considering the blood was not needed to prove Frost had killed Towne, and it did not clear up the premeditation question. But Ball made the point nonetheless. Incidentally, John Rathbone did confirm the castration happened when Frost said it did.

While the legal value of these three points can be debated, the historical value cannot, as they provide a remarkable timeline of events on the Frost farm. Consider just these few facts:

June 30th – Frost's dog kills a woodchuck
July 2nd – Towne kills the newborn calf
July 4th – Frost kills Towne
July 17th - Frost and Rathbone castrate the bull
July 22nd – Frost digs up Towne's body and cuts it into pieces
July 31st – Samuel Upton finds Towne's torso/ Frost arrested/
Carrie examines her brother's decayed skull

To put it mildly, this was not a typical month on a farm in the quiet little town of Petersham, Massachusetts, in 1875. (Nor was it a typical month for an old dog.)

Ball now needed to chip away at Staples' theory on motive. Remember, Ball had promised in his opening to show that Frost was not desperate for money at the time of the murder. He and his client now needed to prove that this was true. So Frost began by admitting he owed John Page and Stephen Goddard the money that the prosecution had shown, but he denied that it was a problem. At the end of each discussion, Ball asked Frost the following:

(Ball) "Had Mr. Page been pressing you for that money hard?"
(Frost) "He had not sir."

(Ball) "Had Mr. Goddard been pressing you for money?"
(Frost) "No sir, he never made any heavy efforts to press me."

Thus, while Frost did have debts to these two, the situation wasn't dire. Just as Frost had admitted to killing Towne but claimed it wasn't murder, he now acknowledged he was in debt, but it wasn't really a problem. It wasn't a compelling argument, but it was the best Ball could do with what he had.

Next Frost addressed his debt to Frank Towne. Samuel had indeed given Frank a note for $325, but not only was that note not pressing, the two men were working their farms and had reason to believe money would soon be coming in, as Ball pointed out:

(Ball) "Were there any crops?"
(Frost) "There were what was on the Page place, what I had about the place. On the 4th of July the crops belonged to Mr. Towne."

(Ball) "Now what would the crops be worth on the Page place? What would you have to pay Mr. Page?"

(Frost) "I don't know how much, for I came away before the crops got farmed over."

(Ball) "How much hay was there on the Frost farm this year?"

(Frost) "I could not say for I had not farmed it all when I came away."

(Ball) "How much was there in the barn when you came away?"

(Frost) "I should say there was about from ten to twelve tons that was cut on the Frost place."

Ball wanted to show that the two best friends were quietly working their farms in the summer of 1875, and things were right on schedule. Further, Towne hadn't been pressing Frost for money because he'd been busy with his farming that year and that work was about to pay off for him with all that hay he had. The problem with the argument was that Towne was the sole owner of his crops whereas Frost was not, and Towne had much more to show for his labors than did Frost. Further, Frost had debts, whereas Towne did not.

Ball had tried his best, but he failed to deliver on his promise regarding Frost's finances. The key question he needed to ask Samuel but couldn't was, "how are you planning to pay these gentlemen back?" Ball needed to convince the jury that Samuel had a plan for settling his affairs outside of murdering Towne, but the reality was that Samuel didn't have such a plan. Whatever money he made off the Page farm that year was certainly going to fall short of what he needed, and Ball couldn't explain how Frost would make up the difference. But Staples could explain it — by Frost murdering Towne.

Before he finished, Ball wanted to attack the premeditation narrative one more time, and so he closed with these three questions:

(Ball) "Now previous to the 4th of July, had you formed any intention of killing Frank Towne?"

(Frost) "No sir."

(Ball) "Did you intend to kill Frank Towne when you went to the barn on that Sunday morning?"

(Frost) "I had no more thought of it than I have of killing myself now."

(Ball) "Did you at any time?"

(Frost) "No sir."

They were the right questions to end with, and Frost had given the only answers he could. Those three questions were at the very heart of Frost's defense, and the believability of those three answers would determine what would happen to the very soul of Samuel J. Frost.

Then it was the prosecution's turn with the defendant:

(Staples) "What business had you there anyway in that barn?"

The District Attorney asked a great question. After all, both the farm and the livestock in the barn belonged to Towne. Frost's responsibilities lay not in the barn but on the Page farm that he was renting. Further, Samuel had already testified that Towne hadn't asked him for any help that morning. In fact, Towne expressly stated (in Frost's version) that he would prefer to milk all the cows, which is what led to the alleged fight in the first place. So Staples' question was spot on — *what was Frost doing in there* so early in the morning when his presence was neither needed nor wanted?

(Staples) "What business had you there anyway in the barn?"
(Frost) "What business?"
(Staples) "That morning, with the cows?"
(Frost) "I went in there to milk that cow."
(Staples) "What was that to you? Had you any rights over the cow?"
(Frost) "I had no more right, not in one sense, than anyone else had. Not supposing I had been forbidden, but being as I had been in the habit of doing it, of milking her, I went in that morning."
(Staples) "If I understand you all right, you said that it was proposed that Frank should let you milk that cow on Friday, he readily assented and you milked her?"
(Frost) "Yes sir."
(Staples) "Also Saturday morning?"
(Frost) "Yes sir."
(Staples) "But this Sunday morning, all this arose because he was not willing that you should milk that cow?"
(Frost) "Yes sir."
(Staples) "That is your statement?"
(Frost) "Yes sir."

Frost's answers made little sense. Without having been asked by Towne to milk the heifer, he went into the barn out of habit, a habit formed over just two days. In those two days, Towne had readily accepted the help of Frost. But now, on this third day, Towne was not only not receptive to Frost's assistance, he was ready to physically fight him over it? Remember, Carrie Frost had testified that in the ten years the two men had known each other they had never once come to blows. It all seemed unlikely.

Staples had picked up on several other inconsistencies with Frost's testimony, starting with the mysterious Mr. Whitehouse:

> (Staples) "Do I understand you to say that Mr. Whitehouse actually bargained for your farm?"
> (Frost) "I did sir."
> (Staples) "To take half of it?"
> (Frost) "To take half of it, yes sir."
> (Staples) "Did you hear him testify here today?"
> (Frost) "I did sir."

Staples let that hang for several seconds, knowing that the jury would remember Whitehouse testifying that he had never gotten back to Frost about buying the farm. Either Frost was lying or Whitehouse was, and either scenario was bad for Frost.

Staples next went after Ball's assertion that Frost didn't have pressing financial concerns:

> (Staples) "Had you any means of settling with Mrs. Cook after you knew of her entry of foreclosure on the farm? Had you any means to go and pay your interest to Mr. Goddard, or your installment?"
> (Frost) "I had no money about me with which to do it."
> (Staples) "Had you any prospect?"
> (Frost) "I could have raised it."
> (Staples) "Did you make any attempt to raise it?"
> (Frost) "No sir."
> (Staples) "Did you raise it?"
> (Frost) "I raised it after Mr. Towne disappeared."
> (Staples) "How?"
> (Frost) "By mortgaging cows and a horse to Mr. Page."
> (Staples) "Those belonged to Mr. Towne?"

(Frost) "They did sir."

(Staples) "Well, at the time, that Sunday morning, the 4th of July, when this affair took place, you knew then about this entry to foreclose?"

(Frost) "I did sir."

Staples needn't have continued after that exchange. Those seven questions showed that Frost was fully aware of his precarious hold on his farm, he had no means to meet his financial obligations prior to the 4th, and he was only able to do so after the 4th by using the murdered Towne's possessions. Had Staples wanted to get snarky, he might then have stated, "Well, what a lucky break for you Mr. Frost, that Frank Towne 'disappeared' just when you needed him to." But Staples wasn't that kind of attorney, and he knew full well that the jury was already thinking along those lines. Plus, he wanted to follow up on the Page mortgage of July 8th:

> (Staples) "What made you mortgage that stock of Mr. Towne's to raise money?"
>
> (Frost) "I did it to kind of deceive people's eyes, more than any thing else."
>
> (Staples) "What about?"
>
> (Frost) "About Mr. Towne's disappearing sir. I thought I would make them believe I hired that money to pay him off with. That is what I told Mr. Page."
>
> (Staples) "Then your object in mortgaging that stock was not to get money?"
>
> (Frost) "It was not precisely to get the money."
>
> (Staples) "You say "not precisely". Was it any part of your object to get the money?"
>
> (Frost) "Yes sir."
>
> (Staples) "To do what with?"
>
> (Frost) "To pay Mr. Goddard."

This was Frost's worst answer of the day. Nobody believed he got that money "to deceive people's eyes." Everybody believed he needed that money to pay Goddard. Staples had yet again driven home premeditation, and he'd made Frost look foolish in the process.

Before he finished, Staples wanted to get Frost on the record talking about the issue Ball purposely did not — what happened to the body after Frost had noticed the Rathbone boys snooping around:

(Staples) "Did you draw that body to that swamp?"
(Frost) "I did not."
(Staples) "Never?"
(Frost) "Never."
(Staples) "Did you draw that body down that lane?"
(Frost) "I did not."
(Staples) "Did you have your cattle out in the night between ten and two o'clock?"
(Frost) "I did not."
(Staples) "Between the 4th of July and the day of your arrest?"
(Frost) "I did not."
(Staples) "Were you out yourself any night between ten and two o'clock?"
(Frost) "I was sir."
(Staples) "Were you out another night from about ten till about daybreak?"
(Frost) "I was out one night."
(Staples) "But one?"
(Frost) "I was out one night from two o'clock till three o'clock. I was sir, and I was out one night from one o'clock until half past three o'clock. That was the night that I moved that body out from under the barn, sir."
(Staples) "Do you remember what day of the month that was?"
(Frost) "I do not sir, but I can explain it…"
(Staples) "I will ask you this, was it the night you recollect that Mr. Upton came there, the Chairman of the Selectmen?"
(Frost) "Yes sir."
(Staples) "Did you have the oxen out that night?"
(Frost) "I did not sir."

Surprisingly Staples stopped there. The exchange seemingly begged for follow up questions like, "Where did you move the body to?" and "How did you move the body if not with oxen?" Staples didn't ask because he felt the jury knew the answers to those questions. Also surprising was that the DA never asked Frost when and how he cut up Towne's body. After all, it was the butchering of the corpse that had made the trial such a sensation in the first place. Further, it would seem a natural end point, as it would remind the jury of that awful thing Frost had done.

But again, Staples wasn't quite as interested in the sensationalism of the crime as was the public.

Regardless, the District Attorney had done plenty of damage to Frost. The re-direct lasted only a minute. Attorney Hopkins did not bother trying to refute anything Staples had just pointed out, but instead he tried to clarify an insignificant detail about where in the stone wall a hatchet and blanket were found. It was a strange place to conclude the defendant's testimony, but that is how it ended.

As to how Frost did, with 150 years of hindsight (and knowing the outcome of the trial), it's easy to see where his testimony came up short. But in the moment, the reviews were actually quite favorable. For example, the *Worcester West Chronicle* offered this:

> Frost was on the stand for three hours, and not once did he show the least sign of nervousness. His story seemed to be well prepared, and he stood the cross-examination without faltering.

The *Boston Post* agreed in its much more descriptive critique:

> Great interest in the evidence given by the defendant was manifested throughout. Especially was this shown when in the cross-examination the defendant stepped down from the witness stand and lying prostrate on the floor explained the manner of striking the blow by which Towne came to his death. His answers to the questions of counsel were delivered in a most positive manner, and he seemed relieved when the examination was through. The voice of the prisoner, which was at first almost inaudible, rose at last till every word he said could be distinctly heard in every part of the room.

And *The Worcester Daily Spy* added this interesting aside:

> Once or twice he attempted to put on an exhibition of bravado, and to speak sharply to the district attorney, but he soon checked himself and renewed his usual self-possession.

If those assessments were any indication, the defense had some reason to be optimistic.

Incidentally, there was one part of Frost's testimony that was not mentioned in the papers, but had it played out just a little differently it might well have been the headline. During his initial questioning, Ball *did* actually ask Samuel something that everyone who'd been following the case wanted him to ask. The exchange took place after Samuel spoke of having eaten very little for breakfast following Towne's murder:

> (Ball) "What was the condition of your mind at that time?"
> (Staples) "Oh, that is of no consequence."
> (Frost) "I could not explain it."
> (Staples) "No matter sir." (To Ball) "Go on."
> (Ball) "What did you do after you rose from the table?"
> (Frost) "I went and sat down in the north door of the house."

Legally, what Frost was thinking was irrelevant, so Staples was technically right to interject. But *everyone* other than Staples desperately wanted to know what Frost would have said had he been pressed to answer. It was the one time the people of Massachusetts (and history) wished that Staples *hadn't* done his job.

Frost's attorney John Hopkins
(As printed in *The Worcester Magazine* in August of 1902)

12

The Closing Arguments

The trial's final day began at 9:00am Friday morning. Ball began by recalling John Rathbone and Coroner Shattuck for quick and unnecessary clarifications. He then introduced a doctor's note stating that Frost's neighbor, Mr. Loring, was unfit to testify. Staples offered no objection, as he couldn't have cared less if Loring testified or not. Following those brief items, this exchange occurred:

(Ball) "The defendant closes his case here."
(Colt) "Does the government have anything in reply?"
(Staples) "We have nothing in reply."
(Colt) "Is the defense ready to give its closing statement?"
(Hopkins) "Yes your honors."

At the outset of the trial, attorney Hopkins had shown a penchant for being long-winded, as when he made his case for a change of venue. That initial argument, it turned out, was but an appetizer. As Hopkins rose to begin, no one in the courtroom could have known that he would talk for SIX HOURS in closing the defense's case. His closing would end up being twice as long as Frost's actual testimony! But what Hopkins' close lacked in brevity, it more than made up for in style. Hopkins was about to show why he had the reputation of being one of the best defense attorneys in the state. He began:

On behalf of the prisoner at the bar we do not claim that he is guiltless of having killed Frank Towne, but we do not admit the crime charged in the indictment. What we admit is manslaughter, and that is a lesser crime than murder. The question for you to decide is: did Mr. Towne die from the affects of a blow delivered in a quarrel or from premeditated malice? No mortal eye but his own saw what took place in that barn that Sunday morning. Fortunately, the law allows him to tell his own story, and we think he has told you the whole truth.

The defense's first objective had always been to get a manslaughter verdict, so naturally Hopkins started there. He then needed to remind the jury of the legal clarification Ball had made to them in his opening:

> Now the question is, was the homicide committed with deliberation and malice? With ill will or cruelty or atrocity? What does "cruelty and atrocity" mean? It means that what was done at the time of the commission of the crime and NOT what was done with the body AFTER the death of the victim. The jury will please note the distinction. However much you may have found the body of Towne mutilated after death, you are to forget it as part of the crime with which the prisoner stands charged.

Frost could only hope the jury would heed Hopkins' words, but forgetting the butchering of Towne's body was much easier said than done, regardless of what the law instructed.

Next, he tried a new tact in going after the prosecution's theory on motive:

> Then there's the labor which Towne performed. It may be claimed that Frost wished to get it for nothing. But the evidence shows that Towne had hired the farm and agreed to pay $200 and the taxes, and at the end of the year Frost would have $200 and his taxes in his pocket. Then at the first of July the crops were in the ground and it would require much labor to gather them, so that on the whole Frost was much worse off in pocket after the homicide than he would have been had Towne lived.

This idea had not been presented during any questioning within the trial. Hopkins' new contention was that not only was Towne not killed for money, his death actually *hurt Frost financially!* Offering such a new theory in his closing suggested that Hopkins knew Ball hadn't succeeded in answering the financial questions during witness testimony. Hopkins then added that Frost was due $300 from the mysterious Mr. Whitehouse, even though Whitehouse testified that he never agreed to pay that figure. Motive had been a problem throughout for the defense, so Hopkins used his closing to try one last time to muddy those waters.

Then Hopkins got nasty. The prosecution had used a star witness, and Hopkins needed to diminish her impact. While he'd been careful not to bully Carrie Frost when she was on the stand, he unloaded with full gusto on her now:

> When Mr. Frost leased his farm to Mr. Towne he then hired another farm, and he was always at work, although his wife comes here with the wickedest heart ever borne in a woman, and says he did not work at all this year. Over the skull of the dead brother she freely tells all the law will allow to tell against her husband. Such brazen effrontery has seldom if ever been seen in a court of justice, and when a woman so far forgets her duty to her husband, the jury may very well doubt her word as to what she states to them.

What the jury thought of *that* can never be known, but there can be no doubt what Hopkins' client thought about it. It was as if Samuel was speaking directly to Carrie through Hopkins, and the vitriol in those words showed just how angry Samuel was because of what his wife had done to him.

Lastly, Hopkins ended his marathon presentation by reminding the jury what was at stake in all of this:

> The counsel have performed an arduous duty, and now you become the principal actors in these proceedings to see whether Samuel J. Frost shall live or die. We ask that you bring in a verdict of manslaughter, as such a verdict would much more subserve the ends of justice than would a verdict of first degree murder, which would consign the prisoner to an ignominious death on the gallows.

Given the constraints of his case, Hopkins had given it his best shot. His argument boiled down to: Frost had indeed killed Towne; it was not premeditated; the prosecution's motive for the killing was weak; their star witness was flawed; and the most revolting aspect of the case had no legal bearing at all. Frost could not have asked for more from his court-appointed attorney. Little did Hopkins and Frost know at the time, but that last line would turn out to be the truest thing Hopkins uttered in the entire trial. (Indeed it would be an "ignominious death on the gallows" for Samuel!)

Now it was the prosecution's turn. At the beginning of the trial, Attorney General Train had gotten the better of Hopkins during the change of venue request, even though Hopkins had argued much longer and much more theatrically. The closings would be déjà vu. Train started with Hopkins' last point:

> The counsel for the defense says the question for you to decide is whether Samuel J. Frost shall live or die. That is NOT for you to say. Our constitution defines the laws under which we live, and each department of our government is defined, and one cannot interfere with the other. You are to find the facts in the case on your oaths, and not say whether Frost shall live or die. Your duty as defined by law is plain, and we doubt not you will conscientiously do it.

Without theatrics, the veteran Attorney General calmly reminded the jury that its job was simply to find the defendant guilty of murder or not. If he was guilty, then it was the legislature that was responsible for Frost's fate, not the jury.

As a legal distinction, Train was right. But the jurors were human beings, they knew full well what the ramification of their decision would be. Hopkins had made a similar legal point in regards to Frost's handling of Towne's body. It may have been shocking, but it was not legally relevant. While Train knew that to be true, he was absolutely going to remind the jury what Samuel had done to Frank's corpse:

> Mr. Frost and Mr. Towne were together Saturday before Towne's death, and went to ride and in bathing (swimming). The next thing we find Frank Towne buried in Frost's barn cellar. The men who lived on the farm discovered the grave and we have it now brought out in the evidence that he, Frost, buried him there. We also have it that there was a man on the earth so destitute of all human feeling that he took his brother-in-law's body, and in the stillness of the night, took a yoke of oxen and dragged that body down a lane and buried it in the swamp. The atrocity and cruelty displayed in disposing of that body are almost unprecedented, and it does not seem possible that it could have been done. Yet the facts are before you, and the defendant is guilty of the offense.

Next, the Attorney General was not going to allow Hopkins'
brutal attack on Carrie Frost to go unchecked:

> Ever since the commission of the crime with which he is
> charged Mr. Frost has lied from the top of his head to the sole
> of his foot. In contrast, Mrs. Frost has been here and told her
> story, and we have shown it to be the truth. And so I ask you,
> which is the better person of the two, Mr. or Mrs. Frost? No
> one ventured to say but that she is as moral, as virtuous, as
> religious a person as there is in this community. Some may
> claim that when a woman marries she sinks all moral rights in
> her husband, but I deny it. A woman owes certain duties to her
> husband, to her children, and to society. She came here, and
> in the interest of society told all that the law would allow her to
> tell.

It was an excellent counter to Hopkins' malevolence. Sadly, Carrie
Frost had left the trial during the lunch break to return to Petersham
to be with her children. Thus, while she had the misfortune of hearing
Hopkins' blistering attack firsthand, she wouldn't know of Train's elo-
quent counter until she read it in the papers the next day.

Then, since Hopkins had gone after Carrie's credibility, Train
went after Samuel's:

> Mr. Frost knew that somebody had been molesting the grave
> (under the barn), and so he decided to remove the body. Did
> he drag it down the lane? He denies that he did. But look at the
> testimony. Human hair was found in the lane, and several wit-
> nesses have sworn that the hair resembled that of Frank Towne.
> The route down the lane is well defined; ferns were broken
> down, bushes were bent over. There was every appearance of
> a grave, and yet this lying prisoner asks you to believe it was a
> woodchuck's hole. Don't you suppose that the farmers of Peter-
> sham know a grave from a woodchuck's hole? The sapling pine
> at the grave bears marks of a well-defined cut, and the prisoner
> says his dog gnawed it? Then do you suppose that Mr. Towne
> would have torn a button off his shirt and broken another in
> hunting a woodchuck? Speaking of Mr. Towne's shirt, when his
> body was found his sleeves were rolled up the same as when he
> was last seen. Do you think he could go through such a strug-

gle as Frost describes (when Frost killed him) and not have his shirt sleeves disturbed?

Train's brilliance was now in full effect. "How stupid does he think we are" was the question he was posing to the jury, and the answer was designed to be, "not that stupid." The case had always boiled down to who was the more believable witness, and Train had all but ended the question right there.

Next came motive. Since Hopkins had argued that the prosecution hadn't proven motive, Train laid it out as specifically as he could:

> Having found a dead man, his body cut up into pieces with the skull broken in, our next question is, "How did he come to his death, and if by violence, who did it? What was the motive for it?" The facts which have been divulged here show a motive, and let us say what it was. From the time Mr. Whitehouse came down to see the farm in May, up to the time Towne's stock was mortgaged to Mr. Page, we see the motive cropping up. Frost was in debt, he had leased his farm to Mr. Towne and had no control on his farm. The mortgage on his farm had been foreclosed, and he must extricate himself from his troubles. His first move was to get Mr. Whitehouse to buy one half of the farm, who would give him $300, which would get him out of difficulty. He failed in this, so his next move was to possess himself of Towne's property. And how does he do it without taking Towne's life? After the murder what did he do? Did he not go to John Page, mortgage Towne's property on his own, and take the money and pay Mr. Goddard the interest money (on the farm)? The transaction was all done on the same day and on one trip. Frost was pressed and he must have money. With the death of Towne he got it.

This point was always the fatal flaw in Frost's defense. Hopkins and Ball simply had no answer to the money question. Frost could be mad at Carrie all he wanted, but it was this timeline of *his* actions that had handcuffed his attorneys throughout the trial. Train ended with this:

> Your duty is plain. You are to find a verdict on the facts. Do your duty to society and justice will be vindicated. We leave the case in your hands, feeling that by the close attention you have

given to the testimony, you are fully acquainted with the facts
we have endeavored to prove.

Train didn't tell them what their verdict should be, but he had made it
perfectly clear. Hopkins had been good (and three times longer), but
Train had been better. Again.

Closing statements were not yet over. There was still one more
to be made, as Justice Colt explained:

> Samuel J. Frost, according to a time-honored custom of this
> court, in cases of this description, you are now informed that
> you have an opportunity to address the jury yourself, in your
> own behalf, if you see fit to do so. It is a matter of your elec-
> tion. If you do not do so, but conclude to leave the case as it has
> been left by your counsel, there will be no prejudicial inference
> drawn from that election.

Frost had nothing to lose. He could say whatever he wanted to the
jury and his would be the last word on the matter. At the very least, he
could look them directly in the eyes to tell them once more that he never intended to kill Frank. He could state unequivocally that he would
be forever sorry that he had killed him. And while the courtroom had
already endured some eight hours of closing arguments, it was ready
to hear anything the defendant wanted to add. Frost cleared his throat
and simply said:

> I leave it to my counsel.

Frost wasn't going to change any juror's mind at that point. Still, how
could it have hurt him to deny the prosecution's premeditation theory
one last time? Why not try and tell a better story about the "arrangement" than Whitehouse had? If nothing else he could have looked the
jurors in the eyes and spoken of his love for his children to try and hu-
manize himself a little. But Samuel had given his story the day before,
and he liked how Hopkins had summed up his thoughts in the closing.
Thus, "I leave it to my counsel."

There was still one more lengthy speech before the jury could
finally get to work on a verdict. Justice Devens needed to give the jury
its official instructions, and it took him almost an hour to do so. His
guidance was straightforward and thorough. If the jury felt Frost's act

was "deliberately premeditated malice aforethought," they were to find Frost guilty of murder in the first degree. The jury didn't need a definition of the phrase, but Devens nonetheless defined it for them: "It is the forward design at some previous period to do the wicked and wrongful act." If instead they believed that Towne's death arose out of "mutual combat," a random fight between the two men, then they were to find Frost guilty only of manslaughter.

Then, at long last Devens turned the case over to the jury. After enduring three full days of witnesses and endless oratories, Samuel's fate was finally in their hands. The time had arrived for them to carefully consider everything that had been presented to them, to thoughtfully weigh each and every piece of evidence, to expertly determine who'd been telling the truth and who'd been lying. While they'd been anxiously anticipating this challenge for some time, the full weight of it bore heavily on them as they filed out of the courtroom to begin their deliberations. And there was every reason to believe that a unanimous verdict was going to take considerable time. It was 6:45pm when they began.

Attorney General Charles Train
(Photo courtesy of the State Library of Massachusetts)

Caleb Strong Gerry
(Photo courtesy of the Harvard Historical Society)

13

The Verdict

The time was 7:15pm. The court clerk had just received a note from the jury stating that they had reached a verdict. They had deliberated for less than half an hour. The news spread throughout the courthouse like wildfire, and the nervous excitement intensified immediately inside the building. But several key players in the trial had stepped out for dinner, fully confident that it would take the jury some time to reach its decision. So while everyone was being located and brought back, people inside the courtroom began to speculate as to what the quick verdict meant. Most took it to mean that Frost was guilty of murder, but the defendant himself was overheard telling his sisters that it was going to be manslaughter. In fact, *The Boston Post* quoted Frost as saying:

> The crowd's waiting to hear me sentenced to be hung, but they will be mistaken. I shall not be hung.

Frost was apparently so confident that he even asked Hopkins about the possibility of getting bail after the manslaughter verdict, so that he could go home and tend to his affairs in Petersham before sentencing. (Imagine Carrie's surprise if Samuel had showed up at home that night!)

It took nearly an hour — twice as long as the jury's deliberations — to get everyone back to the courthouse. But by 8:10, all had returned to their seats, including Colt and Devens. Sheriff Bothwell opened the door to the jury room, and in walked the twelve men who had decided whether Samuel J. Frost was to live or die. The first man to walk through the doorway was Caleb Strong Gerry, the jury foreman. Gerry was from the town of Harvard, where he'd been both a Selectmen and a member of the state House of Representatives. Next was Caleb Taft Richardson of Uxbridge, a landowner who'd also been a Selectmen in his town. Third was Eli Howe Merriam, one of the most prominent businessmen in the town of Westminster, where he owned a very successful grain and flour mill. John N. Albee of Worcester was fourth; he had done very well for himself in the woolen textiles industry, and he was currently working as a manager for the Hopeville Manufacturing Company. Next was Reuben Champion, who would later become a Constable in Worcester. Then came George F. Emery, a carpenter who had previously served three years in the Civil War as a member of the Westborough Rifle Company. Edward Bigelow of Rutland was next, he would eventually own the largest retail dairy farm in Worcester. The eighth man to walk through the door was Dudley Stratton, who just three months later would be named the chief engineer for the Leominster Fire Department. Ninth was Elisha Chapin, who had left his pregnant wife to tend to the farm back in Upton during the trial. Samuel S. Pratt of Charlton was next, followed by W.A. Stone of Worcester, and then M.W. Chandler (who mysteriously had no town listed for him in the official records) filled the last seat of the jury box. Sheriff Bothwell pulled the door closed behind Chandler and stood at attention.

The courtroom was now completely silent, even though it was filled well beyond capacity in terms of both bodies and excitement. The only audible noise that could be heard was from the people outside in the hall pressing up against the door trying to listen in. After a brief pause to make sure everyone was set, the court clerk broke the silence by loudly announcing, "Samuel J. Frost." The prisoner alone stood. Then the clerk asked:

> (Clerk) "Gentlemen of the jury, have you agreed upon your verdict?"
> (Gerry) "We have."
> (Clerk) "Prisoner, look at the foreman. Foreman, look at the prisoner. What say you, Mr. Foreman, is Samuel J. Frost guilty or not guilty?"

Frost was staring directly at Gerry. Half of the spectators were also looking at Gerry, while the other half zeroed in on Frost, hoping to catch his reaction the second Gerry uttered the verdict. Frost's sisters, seated in the front row, clasped their white-knuckled hands together for support as they stared at the floor. Their hearts were filled with hope, but their faces were awash in fear. At that moment they appeared to be far more scared than their brother was. As for Frost, he stood firm in the prisoner's box staring at the jury foreman as instructed. Gerry stared back at Frost and did not hesitate in announcing:

"He is guilty, guilty of murder in the first degree."

There was no audible reaction from the crowd, but smiles had crept up on many of their faces. They were long convinced Frost was guilty of murder, yet in the moments before Gerry spoke, doubt had crept in as to what the foreman might say. Gerry's words were validation to them, and they could now breathe comfortably. As for the spectators who were watching to see Frost's reaction, they were disappointed. *The Fitchburg Sentinel* described it this way the next day:

> He received the sentence in the same indifferent manner with which he has regarded all the proceedings since his arrest.

It was not the reaction of someone who had just been wronged. It was the reaction of a hardened man who had braced himself for bad news. Little did he know, there was more to come.

As Frosts' sisters sat in stunned silence, the clerk asked the jury as a whole if this was their verdict, and they nodded in affirmation. Then Attorney General Train immediately rose to speak:

> If the Court please, as the Superior Court, begun at Fitchburg in this county of Worcester on the 2nd Sunday of August last, the Grand Inquest of the body of this county returned an indictment against Samuel J. Frost, of Petersham, for the murder of Frank P. Towne. That indictment was duly certified by the Clerk of the Superior Court into this Court, a copy was served upon the Chief Justice of this Court, upon the Attorney General of the Commonwealth, and upon the prisoner at the bar. He was thereupon arraigned in this court, and pleaded to the indictment that he was not guilty. Learned and able counsel of his own suggestion were assigned to him for his defense. Tuesday morning last was assigned for the trial, a trial has been had, he has been defended with remarkable faithfulness and fidelity, and the jury have returned upon their oaths that he is guilty of murder in the first degree. No exceptions have been taken to any ruling of the Court, I know of no reason why sentence should be delayed, and therefore I move that sentence be now pronounced upon the defendant.

The jury had literally just pronounced Frost guilty, and Train was already trying to move to sentencing. Due to the late hour, Hopkins assumed that sentencing would wait until the following morning. As such, he rose to object to Train's request:

> May it please your Honors, I had hoped that the Attorney General would not move for sentence tonight. The verdict of the jury has followed quite quickly upon the presentation and the submission to them, and their finding is to the counsel for the defendant a surprise. It is unexpected, and we do not feel that we have had that time for consultation and for deliberation as to what it is proper for us to do in the premises. And we ask that this motion of the Attorney General may not be granted or passed upon tonight, and that time may be granted us that we may deliberate and see what, in the interest of the defendant at the bar, we ought to do.

Hopkins was clearly flummoxed, but Train was not. Before Justice Colt could speak, Train offered the following:

> I can only say, may it please your Honors, that there are no rights reserved to the defendant which are not as well reserved to the defendant to him after sentence as before. I can see no occasion for keeping this court here another day to give counsel an opportunity to consult in relation to measures which may as well be taken after sentence as before.

Scrambling, Hopkins tried to counter Train's statement, but Train was having none of it:

> (Hopkins) "I suppose, if your Honors please, that a motion for a new trial would hardly be proper after sentence."
> (Train) "Any time within a year."
> (Colt) "Are there any statute provisions in regard to a motion for a new trial?"
> (Train) "The provision is that it may be granted within a year."
> (Colt) "Have you examined those provisions, Mr. Hopkins?"
> (Hopkins) "No, your Honor, I have not."
> (Colt) "I will give you an opportunity now to do so."

It was not what Hopkins was hoping to hear. With all eyes on him, he was forced to read the brief statute in question. When he'd finished, he dejectedly succumbed to Train's will:

> I find that my impression was wrong in regard to my rights, and that our rights would be safe even if sentence passed at the present time.

The trial had started with Hopkins getting beaten by Train on a legal point, and it was now ending in the same fashion. At the outset Hopkins had taken the court by surprise with his change of venue request, but ultimately he lost that argument. Now it was he who had been taken by surprise, and again he'd come up short. And while the first dispute demonstrated to all his legal abilities, this last argument showed just how beaten he was by the end.

Meanwhile, Justice Colt was not going to make anyone stay in Worcester for another night unnecessarily. He first addressed the newly convicted prisoner:

> (Colt) "Samuel J. Frost, have you any reason to offer why the sentence which the law pronounces against your offense should not now be pressed?"
> (Frost) "I leave it to my counsel, sir."

Frost hadn't spoken up when afforded the opportunity prior to the jury getting the case, so he wasn't about to say anything after they'd convicted him. And what could he say at that point anyway? As for Colt, everyone knew what he was going to say next, but once again, a pin drop could be heard inside that courtroom. After first reiterating that Frost had been given the fairest of trials and stating that he had been afforded every opportunity to defend himself, Colt imposed the court's punishment:

> Stand up, Mr. Frost, if you please. (Frost rose in the prisoner's box.) The jury have returned the verdict against you as guilty of murder in the first degree. It is proper for the Court to say that this verdict is entirely satisfactory. It is useless for me or for the Court to dwell longer upon the details of this offense; and it remains therefore, only for the Court to pronounce upon you the sentence which the law imposes for the grievous crime of which

you stand convicted. (The sheriff then rapped three times, and everyone in the courtroom rose.) And that sentence is, that you, Samuel J. Frost, be removed from this place and detained in close custody in the prison of this county, and from thence that you be taken, at such time as the Executive Government of this Commonwealth may by their warrant appoint, to the place of execution, and that there you be hung by the neck until you are dead. And may God, of his infinite mercy and goodness, have mercy upon you.

With those last words, the case of *Commonwealth v. Samuel J. Frost* was officially over. Barring a miracle, so was Samuel J. Frost.

The Boston Daily Globe.

VOL. VIII., NO. 92.   BOSTON, SATURDAY MORNING, OCTOBER 16, 1875.   EASTERN SPECIAL   PRICE THREE CENTS.

TRIED AND CONVICTED.

Frost, the Petersham Murderer, Found
Guilty of Murder in the
First Degree.

ARGUMENTS OF COUNSEL ON
BOTH SIDES.

SCENES IN THE COURT-ROOM WHILE
WAITING FOR THE VERDICT.

The Terrible Sentence Pronounced — Possibility of a New Trial — Frost's
Demeanor, Etc., Etc.

[Special Despatch to The Boston Globe.]

WORCESTER, Mass., October 15. — The trial of Samuel J. Frost, who murdered his brother-in-law in Petersham last July, was resumed this morning, before a crowd fully equal to any yet seen in court. There was no evidence of importance to be presented to-day, and after recalling a few witnesses the senior counsel for the defence, Mr. Hopkins, addressed the jury in behalf of his client. It was an earnest plea for the wretched man and was listened to with breathless attention. The Attorney-General followed in his usually vigorous style, and the Judge summed up, giving the case to the jury. After an hour's absence they returned, bringing in a verdict of murder in the first degree.

Mr. Hopkins's Plea—Frost's Life and Character.

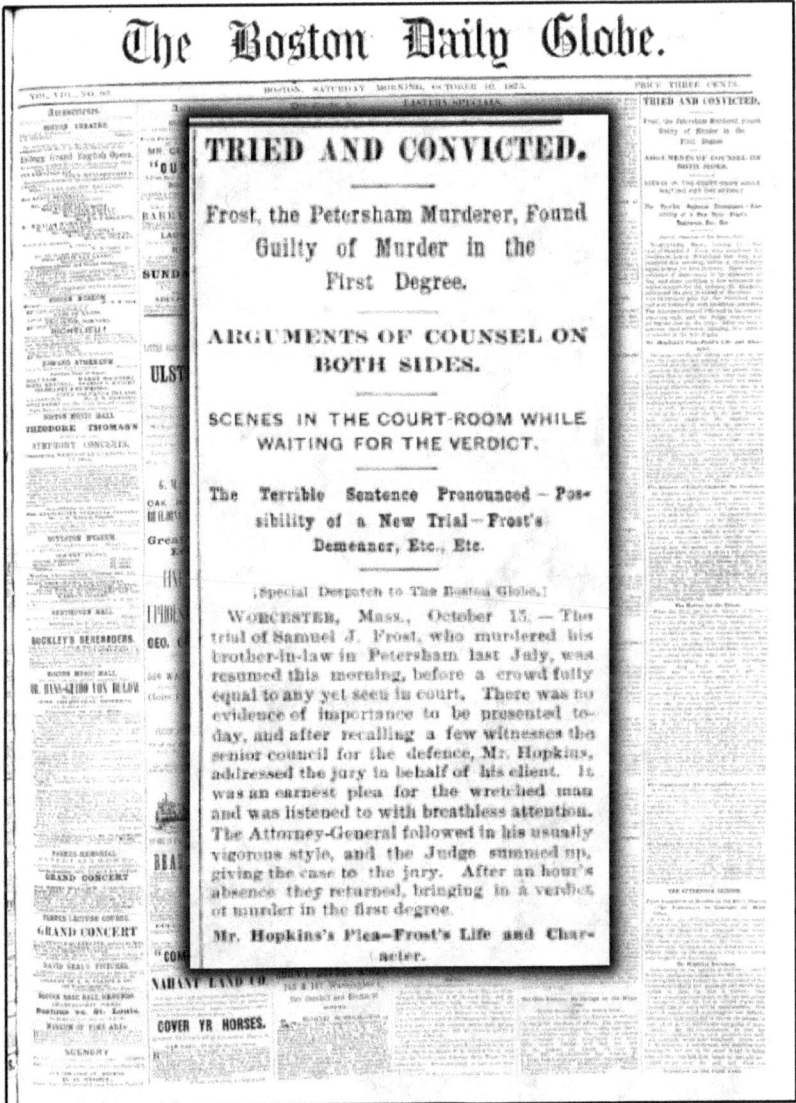

The front page of *The Boston Daily Globe* on October 16, 1875.
(Courtesy of newspapers.com)

Professor C. O. Thompson
(Photo courtesy of wp.wpi.edu)

14

The Leftovers

The trial of the year in Massachusetts was now over. It had come down to two simple questions: *whom* did the jury believe and *what* did the jury believe. Resoundingly they trusted the wife's story over the husband's, and clearly they were sold on premeditation versus spur-of-the-moment death. But as is so often the case in high profile trials such as this, there were a number of ancillary things that happened in it which made *Commonwealth v. Frost* that much more interesting. And from a historical perspective, these side stories help to paint an even clearer picture of the 1875 world in which Frost and Towne existed.

The Cat

Almost as soon as the public first learned of the murder on the Frost farm, they also heard about the story involving the cat. Both *The Fitchburg Sentinel* and *The Boston Post* of August 3rd mentioned it, as did *The Athol Transcript* a few days later:

> The Rathbone boys were a constant source of annoyance to him. He threatened to "fix them," and last Saturday forenoon asked John the younger boy to go down into an old unused well to get out the cat, as it was missing, and he thought it was there. The bait did not take.

The story only grew from there, as papers across the country told of the plan Frost had to kill John Rathbone by luring him down into an abandoned well with the ruse of a fallen cat. When the trial began, the prosecution made the story a significant part of its case. In fact, Staples stated this in his opening:

> He tried to get one of the Rathbone boys to go down into an unused well to get a cat which he said was down there the Saturday before the discovery of the dead body, and who doubts

but what if he had gone? He too would have shared the same fate as Towne.

The District Attorney stated as fact that Frost wanted to kill Rathbone in that well. And when Staples had John Rathbone in the witness box, he pursued the story:

> (Staples) "I want to ask you about the cat in the well business. When was that?
> (Rathbone) "That was on Saturday before he was taken."
> (Staples) "Now state what he said to you, if anything. Did Mr. Frost say anything to you about it?"
> (Rathbone) "Not until he came out. Before he sent someone out to get me."
> (Staples) "Did you go?"
> (Rathbone) "I did not."
> (Staples) "Then what happened? Did he come out after that?"
> (Rathbone) "He came out there in an hour or so afterwards."
> (Staples) "What happened then?"
> (Rathbone) "I got to blowing him about it. I was asking him how he got along about getting the cat out. He says, 'Very well.' Then he says, 'You are all the means of letting this thing out. You will be sorry for it sometime,' says he."

Staples dramatically paused on that last line, "you will be sorry for it sometime." The story made Frost out to be even more of a monster, as he was obviously willing to kill again to cover his tracks. It was very effective, and the public had eaten up the story. But it was nonsense.

When Carrie Frost was in the witness box, John Hopkins questioned her about the cat story. Her version was quite different than the sensationalized version implied by DA Staples:

> (Hopkins) "Have you got a well under your kitchen?"
> (Carrie) "Yes sir."
> (Hopkins) "How deep is it from the kitchen floor to the top of the water?"
> (Carrie) "I don't know."
> (Hopkins) "Do you remember the fact of missing a kitten one morning?"
> (Carrie) "Yes sir, I do."

(Hopkins) "Do you remember the fact that you sought for it some time and could not find it?"

(Carrie) "Yes sir."

(Hopkins) "Do you remember the fact that your husband found it in the well?"

(Carrie) "No sir, I found it myself."

(Hopkins) "You found it there yourself. Do you remember sending for your husband?"

(Carrie) "Yes sir."

(Hopkins) "Do you remember his sending your boy for John Rathbone?"

(Carrie) "Yes sir."

(Hopkins) "Do you remember getting word that John Rathbone would not come up?"

(Carrie) "Yes sir, my little boy brought that word."

(Hopkins) "So your little boy was there?"

(Carrie) "Yes sir."

(Hopkins) "What did your husband do to extricate the kitten?"

(Carrie) "He went down into the well and took it out."

(Hopkins) "And you were present, and your little boy too?"

(Carrie) "Yes sir."

(Hopkins) "And at the time John was sent for, your family was up and about the house?"

(Carrie) "Yes sir."

With that Hopkins destroyed the cat story. Carrie had found the missing cat that morning (this was on the 31st, just twelve hours before Towne's torso was found), and she'd she sent for her husband to get it out. But Samuel didn't want to be bothered — he obviously had other things on his mind at that moment — so he sent for John Rathbone, who he'd hired to do chores like that. When Rathbone balked, Frost begrudgingly did it himself. He wasn't intending to kill Rathbone in that well. Had he been, he would not have had his wife and son there with him awaiting Rathbone's arrival. In this instance, Frost's actions were completely innocent and reasonable. But what the cat story did show was that Staples was not above manipulating facts to fit his narrative. (Conversely, AG Train avoided any mention of the cat in his closing.) It also showed that if indeed Carrie wanted Samuel hanged, as Hopkins had argued, she wasn't willing to manipulate the cat story to help her achieve that end.

The Little Girl

The cat legend did bring with it an interesting side detail: while
the Frosts did have a dog, they did not own any cats. Yet there was
indeed a cat in their well that Samuel did have to rescue that day. So
whose cat was it? As a lead-in to her testimony on the cat story, Carrie
mentioned the following:

> (Hopkins) "Had you anyone to assist you about your work be-
> sides John Rathbone?"
> (Carrie) "Yes sir."
> (Hopkins) "Who?"
> (Carrie) "A little girl. Amelia Alexander."
> (Hopkins) "How old a girl?"
> (Carrie) "Twelve."
> (Hopkins) "A relative of yours or your husband's?"
> (Carrie) "Neither."
> (Hopkins) "How long was she with you?"
> (Carrie) "Two weeks."
> (Hopkins) "When did she go away?"
> (Carrie) "The day that Mr. Frost was arrested."
> (Hopkins) "So she was with you for the two weeks preceding his
> arrest?"
> (Carrie) "Yes sir."

The cat belonged to that little girl, Amelia Alexander.

But what was Amelia doing in the Frost house in the first place?
As it happened, Amelia had gotten sick (Carrie thought she had a slight
case of typhoid fever), and Carrie had agreed to take her in until she
recovered, presumably for a small fee. How Carrie knew of Amelia's
plight is unclear, but one possibility is that she knew her from church.
In any case, Amelia had brought two kittens with her when she came to
stay with the Frosts', and one of those kittens ended up in the well.

What is most intriguing about Amelia is the timing of her visit.
The sick little girl had arrived at the Frost house on or around July 17th,
just two weeks after Towne had been murdered. By that time Carrie
was already convinced that her husband had killed Frank, and she had
witnessed Samuel acting strangely for some time. In spite of that however, Carrie still decided to accept Amelia into her house amidst all that
chaos. (While this seems mind-boggling today, it apparently wasn't in
1875, as neither attorney questioned her about it.) And Amelia didn't

leave the Frost house until August 1st, the day Frost was arrested. As if there hadn't been enough craziness on that farm already, Samuel's last day as a free man started with him climbing into a well to rescue a kitten which belonged to a sick little girl who had no business being in his house. Then that day ended with a black man who had never been on Frost's farm until that very day finding the partial remains of the murder victim.

The Widow Snow

There was absolutely no need for Eunice Snow to testify in Samuel J. Frost's trial, but history is glad she did. She was a prosecution witness, and her entire testimony consisted of just seven questions:

(Staples) "You live in Petersham?"
(Snow) "Yes sir."
(Staples) "Did you know Mr. Towne?"
(Snow) "I have seen him."
(Staples) "Franklin P. Towne?"
(Snow) "I did know him by sight."
(Staples) "Do you recollect seeing him on or near the fourth July last?"
(Snow) "He called at my house on the third evening of July."
(Staples) "On the third evening of July?"
(Snow) "Yes sir."
(Staples) "How long did he stay there?"
(Snow) "I should think about ten minutes."
(Staples) "What time was it in the evening?"
(Snow) "Just at dusk."

And that was it. The defense waived its cross-examination of Eunice, and she was done. In some minor way she helped add to the defense's timeline for the victim in the hours leading up to his death. But it had long been established that he was alive on the evening of the third, so she really added nothing.

But Eunice Snow simply belonged in the most famous trial in the history of Petersham. After all, Eunice was herself famous in those parts at the time. Her celebrity derived not so much from who she was, but rather who her husband was — "Popcorn" Snow. When "Popcorn" (real name Asa) died in 1872, he left behind a legacy of peculiarity that trailed his widow long after his death. Eunice's husband had earned his nickname via his diet. He considered himself a vegetarian, and his diet was said to consist almost exclusively of two things – popcorn and milk. Legend had it that he loved popcorn so much that he'd left instructions to have his casket filled with it upon his death! Besides popcorn, Eunice's husband also loved money. Thus, even though he himself never ate meat, "Popcorn" earned a living by selling beef and pork. In a strange twist of fate, it was pork that actually killed the vegetarian. He suffered a fatal heart attack in late November of 1872 while trying to drag a dressed pig carcass up to his house during a heavy snowstorm. While Popcorn's death had been ironic, his afterlife would make him famous.

In life "Popcorn" had developed a fear of being buried alive. As a result, prior to his death he'd made specific arrangements to insure that his fears were not realized. First, he paid a local coffin-maker a large sum to custom-build a metal casket for him, which was most unusual at the time. Next, he instructed the man to insert a ten-inch square glass window at the head of the coffin, so that his face could be viewed from above. Finally, he arranged to have the local undertaker visit his body in the coffin for seven days after his death to insure that he was indeed dead. Only then, according to "Popcorn's" specific instructions, could he be laid in the ground. When "Popcorn" died, the undertaker attempted to hold up his end of the bargain. Despite the region being hit with a massive snowstorm, he rode out to the Snows for the first two days to check on the presumed dead man. On the third day however, while en route amidst even more snow and freezing temperatures, Eunice stopped the undertaker and told him to forget the whole thing. She sent him home, supposedly with the words, "If he wasn't dead when they put him in there, he's surely frozen by now." Some three years after sending her husband to his final resting place a bit early, Eunice Snow played a *tiny* role in doing the same to her neighbor, Samuel J. Frost.

(Much of the above information on Popcorn Snow was taken from J.R. Greene's excellent book *Strange Tales From Old Quabbin*, Highland Press.)

The Sexton

Like Eunice Snow, Thomas Aldrich testified only briefly in the trial. He was the sexton (gravedigger) for the southern part of Petersham, and most likely he was the man who put "Popcorn" Snow's metal coffin in the ground. Thomas Aldrich was called to testify that he'd dug the grave for Frank Towne's body on August 1st, and then he'd exhumed the grave in late September so that Sheriff Bothwell could take Towne's skull to the trial. But what makes Aldrich's testimony noteworthy is his answer to the second question asked of him:

> (Staples) "You live in Petersham?"
> (Aldrich) "I do."
> (Staples) "What is your occupation?"
> (Aldrich) "Not much of anything."

If ever there was a line that summed up the mindset of a gravedigger in small-town New England in 1875, Aldrich's answer was it. Remember, this trial was a sensation. It was being written about in newspapers across the country, and people were trying anything they could to get inside the courtroom just so they could say they were there. Thus, anyone involved in the trial was keenly aware that *everyone* was watching. As such, no one would have admonished Aldrich if he embellished his answer just a little and replied, "farmer", or maybe "farmhand", or even "I do a little of this and a little of that." But Thomas Aldrich couldn't have cared less. He was what he was, and that was that. So while there were two Supreme Judicial Court Justices sitting behind him and the Attorney General of the Commonwealth sitting in front of him, Thomas Aldrich had no problem answering that question with, "not much of anything." He was much more concerned about getting Towne's skull back after the trial so that he could re-bury it before the ground froze. Such was the thinking of a Petersham sexton in 1875.

The 'Brilliant' Scientist

Everything Thomas Aldrich wasn't, Dr. Charles O. Thompson was. Seven years prior to the trial, Thompson had been named President of the newly formed Worcester County Free Institute of Industrial Science, now known as WPI. It was a first-of-its-kind college devoted almost exclusively to the sciences, and Thompson was a perfect fit for the institution. He loved to talk science with anyone who'd listen, and over time he had found his services being requested more and more in criminal trials. The chemistry professor was all too happy to use a trial's platform to espouse the virtues of the new developments in forensic science. *Commonwealth v. Frost* provided him with an excellent opportunity to do just that. DA Staples was very excited to have him as a witness, and he questioned Dr. Thompson at length about the blood-soaked wood chips taken from the Frost barn:

> (Staples) "What is your occupation sir?"
>
> (Thompson) "I am a scientist."
>
> (Staples) "Are you connected with an institution?"
>
> (Thompson) "Yes sir. I am Professor of Chemistry in the Institution on the hill, as it is called."
>
> (Staples) "What do you find here sir, with that which I now show you?"
>
> (Thompson) "I find a chestnut wood chip, coated with manure, with unmistakable drips of blood stain.
>
> (Staples) "Did you subject these stains to any examination or analysis?"
>
> (Thompson) "I have sir."
>
> (Staples) "Will you describe the process that you used?"
>
> (Thompson) "As soon as you find a place that is thick enough to bear a cross section, we pass the thin blade of a knife through it and it will disclose its characteristic color. It looks as red as when it was first drawn. The red color is due to the presence of oxide of iron, which is one of the most permanent substances on Earth. It resists the actions of organic matter very greatly. Air will keep it red, although other agencies might reduce it to magnetic oxide. Furthermore, I succeeded in producing well-characterized fibers of the blood and that confirmed me in my general conviction that this is blood. Furthermore, the quantity of iron in this is unmistakable, and various other collateral facts left no doubt whatever."
>
> (Staples) "Did you make any examination in reference to the corpuscles?"
>
> (Thompson) "I did sir. But I am not willing to declare what the results are. Blood that has been dried as long as that has does not disclose itself, by that test, very satisfactorily."
>
> (Staples) "That test is a test as to what sort of blood it is, is it not?"
>
> (Thompson) "Mainly so. Still the corpuscles of blood are very well characterized, and it will be decided from the character of the substance if they have not been dried."
>
> (Staples) "In this case of dried blood where the test case can be thus applied, those other tests you think are conclusive?"
>
> (Thompson) "Yes sir, there is very little mistake in ascertaining

blood stains."

(Staples) "So that you would not be prepared to go beyond that naked statement? That this stain is in your opinion a blood stain, but when you come to what sort of blood it is, whether the blood of an animal or the blood of a man, that you would not of course feel prepared to say?"

(Thompson) "No sir."

After all the buildup and technical rhetoric, the celebrity scientist sounded no smarter than the unassuming sexton. The blood stain was taken from inside the barn of a working farm, in an area where a bull had recently been castrated, and the furthest Dr. Thompson was willing to go was that the stain was indeed blood. Thomas Aldrich could have told Staples that. But even if Dr. Thompson could have proved that the blood in the barn was human blood, so what? The defense had conceded that Frost killed Towne in the barn, so it stood to reason there would be human blood in there.

Staples had summoned Dr. Thompson to bring some 1875 cutting edge science to the prosecution, but 1875 science wasn't nearly as cutting edge as Staples presumed it would be. Thus, while Thompson hadn't been quite as bad a witness as the mysterious Mr. Whitehouse, he was close. If nothing else, Thompson proved that Staples wasn't perfect; he was just as capable of unnecessary blunders as Hopkins and Ball were.

The Punch Line

Immediately following the trial, reports of the verdict began popping up in newspapers across the country. Under normal circumstances those reports wouldn't warrant a mention, since they were almost always the same item, as typified by *The Galveston Daily News* (Texas) on page 1:

To be Hanged.

Worcester, Mass., Oct. 16 – Samuel
K. Frost, who was on trial for the murder of his brother-in-law, Fred. P. Lowne,
in Petersham, July 4, has been found
guilty and sentenced to be hanged.

Aside from the errors in both Frost's and Towne's names, this was how most of the world received the news of Samuel's fate. It was a simple statement of fact about a trial that ended with a death sentence.

But not *every* newspaper had the story exactly like that. There was a newspaper in Pennsylvania that somehow ended up with a uniquely incorrect spelling of Frank Towne's last name, and as a result the paper played the story for *laughs!* The Altoona Tribune printed its version of the news on November 4th, but because of the erroneous surname it had, the paper decided to add an editorial comment to the item. That line dramatically changed the way its readers were given the otherwise serious news of a murder conviction/death sentence:

> At Worcester, Mass., Samuel J. Frost was
> recently convicted of the murder of F. Toome,
> and sentenced to be hanged. All cold and un-
> feeling puns and grave jokes are prohibited.

This was the lone instance of Towne's last name being mistakenly written as "Toome," and this was the only time the word "jokes" appeared in any article about this case.

The Near Tears

There was one constant from the moment Frank Towne was killed right through Justice Colt's handing down of the death sentence. The constant was that Samuel J. Frost never showed any emotion. (Aside from laughing at Sheriff Bothwell, that is.) He remained hardened throughout the entire ordeal, even as a noose was later placed around his neck. But there was a brief moment during Stephen Goddard's testimony that is worth noting. Goddard was the man Frost paid on July 8th after he'd mortgaged Towne's livestock with John Page. During the transaction, Goddard recalled the following:

> (Staples) "Did he say anything to you at that time in regard to Mr. Towne?"
> (Goddard) "He did, yes. I asked him some questions in regard to him."
> "What did you ask him? What did he say?"
> "I asked him where Frank was, and he said he was in Worcester on Wednesday on Front Street. I asked him where he had stayed in Worcester, and he said he didn't ask Frank where he had stayed, and he told me that he went into one or two places

on Front Street. I cannot say whether he told me the names or
not of the places he visited, but Mr. Towne went in with him
and bought a pair of boots. In mentioning Frank's name at one
time, his voice trembled very much as he called 'Frank.'"

"Was it very marked?"

"It was quite so, yes sir. It trembled very much."

With everything that had been written and said about Samuel over the
past three months, this was the only time anyone ever mentioned his
having shown any sort of remorse or sadness about what had happened to Frank. The prosecution's theory was that Samuel had killed
Frank primarily to stave off foreclosure. Not coincidentally, as Samuel
was doing just that — paying Mary Cook's agent the money he'd just
received for Towne's livestock — his voice trembled as he mentioned
Frank's name. From the moment he'd woken up on July 4th until that
moment on July 8th, Frost had been running on adrenaline. But as that
adrenaline finally wore off, and as he was finally paying some of the
mortgage with his ill-gotten blood money, the reality of his crime finally seemed to hit him. And if indeed that was the reason for his voice
having trembled at that moment, then it would be the only time Samuel
gave even the slightest hint of sadness for what he had done to his best
friend, Frank Towne.

Judge James D. Colt
(Photo courtesy of mass.gov)

15

The Appeal

All was not yet lost for Samuel J. Frost. John Hopkins had hinted at an appeal the night Justice Colt imposed the death sentence on his client, and he was true to his word. On the last day of November 1875, he officially filed a motion for a new trial with the Supreme Judicial Court in Worcester. As printed in *The Worcester Daily Spy*, the appeal was predicated on four objections:

First: That said verdict is against the law and the evidence and the weight of the evidence.

Second: That he has not had a fair and impartial trial in that the jury empaneled for his trial, were, during the time of said trial placed in the care and keeping of one Sylvester Bothwell, a deputy of the sheriff of said county, said Bothwell being the officer by whom he was arrested, and being an important and material witness against him on his said trial.

Third: That the jury by whom he was tried was, during all the time of said trial, in the custody and care of one Sylvester Bothwell, an important and material witness for the Commonwealth upon said trial, and during all the time aforesaid, viz: four days and nights, said witness for the Commonwealth ate with, slept with, and had charge of said jury.

Fourth: That the jury aforesaid, during the progress of said trial, and during the intermission thereof, was supplied with large numbers of the then current issues of all the daily newspaper press, from which all direct allusions to the trial aforesaid had been cut out, but which, nevertheless, contained matter calculated to improperly influence the minds of the jurors against the defendant and his cause.

Hopkins had taken over a month to file his appeal, but he hadn't come up with much in that time. He was not suggesting any new evidence had come to light, nor was he pointing to any procedural negligence that had taken place within the actual trial. Instead, he was just rehashing his change of venue argument while also attempting to essentially put Sheriff Bothwell on trial. Nonetheless, Justices Colt and Devens wanted no second-guessing in how they handled this particular case, so they granted Hopkins' motion. The hearing was set for January 15th in Boston.

The hearing began with Justice Colt summoning three sheriffs before he and Devens so as to address some of the issues at hand. The first of these was Sheriff Sprague. He'd been the one who provided the newspapers to the jury during the trial, so Colt wanted to again hear how exactly the sheriff had handled that. Sprague explained that he and he alone purchased newspapers for the jury. They were kept in his office at the courthouse, and he himself cut out all references to the trial in those newspapers. It seemed a reasonable counter to Hopkins' claim, just as it had been at the time of the trial.

Next was Sheriff Bothwell. He testified that he was indeed in charge of keeping the jury sequestered during the trial, and as part of that duty he did in fact eat and sleep in those same quarters. A small building behind the courthouse had been transformed into a temporary "inn" where the jury had stayed when not in court. Bothwell stayed there as well to ensure that no one approached the jurors for any nefarious reasons. He emphatically told Colt that at no time did he ever talk to anyone on the jury about the case while in those quarters.

Finally, Deputy Sheriff Gould was brought in. He'd assisted Bothwell during that week, and Colt wanted to know if he had seen or heard anything that Bothwell might have missed. He hadn't. He never heard Bothwell speak with the jury about the case, he himself never spoke with any juror about it, and he never saw any newspapers in those quarters that were not cut up. To his knowledge, everything had been done in accordance with the court's instructions.

With that completed, it was time for the legal arguments to be made. Having remembered his theatrics at trial, Colt braced himself as Hopkins rose to speak. The defense attorney began by restating his original closing argument, claiming yet again that the prosecution had failed to prove premeditation. He maintained that the mysterious Mr. Whitehouse never had an agreement with Frost, and without such an agreement there could be no proof of premeditation. Next he argued that the government's theory that Frost had moved the body multiple times was both far-fetched and unproven. Third, he insisted that Frost's actions constituted manslaughter and not murder, because he left the barn door open when he walked in that morning. Surely he would have closed the door if he had predetermined he was going to kill Towne, Hopkins posited. (Of course, had Frost pulled that door shut, Towne would surely have heard it, thus eliminating Samuel's element of surprise as he snuck up behind Frank before striking him.) Hopkins was grasping at straws, and he knew it. But it was all he could do for his client.

He saved his best argument for last, and it pertained to Sheriff Bothwell. *The Worcester Daily Spy* summed it up this way:

> The fact that Deputy Sheriff Bothwell, who was an important government witness, was placed in charge of the jury, a procedure without precedent in this state, and while no claim was made that he had attempted to influence the jury when in charge of them, the fact that he ate and slept with them, and conducted himself properly, his testimony would, as a matter of course, have greater influence on the minds of the jurors than that of Samuel J. Frost, who was prejudged as guilty by the public at large, including the jury.

This was Hopkins' best argument for the appeal. If indeed Bothwell's keeping watch over the jury was *unprecedented*, the court would need to come to terms with that. The jury had been tasked with evaluating the merits of the government's case against the accused, and one of its key witnesses had actually slept in the same room with them for four nights. That did appear to be problematic. There was no reason Deputy Gould couldn't have performed Bothwell's function properly, and he wasn't a witness in the trial. Further, Gould easily could have secured another deputy had he needed assistance. It was a mistake to have used Bothwell in such a way, and Hopkins demanded a new trial as a result of that mistake.

It was now up to Hopkins' old nemesis, Attorney General Train, to refute Hopkins' assertions. He started by dismissively pointing out that Hopkins had not objected to the idea of the jury getting clipped newspapers when Colt ordered it done at the outset of the trial. Had he found the idea so revolting, he surely would have objected then, but he didn't. Then for good measure he added:

> Furnishing newspapers to jurors in murder trials has always
> been practiced in this state since the adoption of the Consti-
> tution, so that no new practice was entered into, and we claim
> that the defendant's counsel has no cause for complaint.

Train's heart was barely in it, as he knew full well Colt was never going
to overturn his own decision to have the papers brought to the jury.
He'd argued the point to play the game, but he knew he'd already won it.
Colt had already indicated as much in his change of venue ruling back
in October.

As to the Bothwell issue, Train calmly submitted the following:

> The fact that Sheriff Bothwell was a witness for the government
> did not make him incompetent to act as an officer in charge of
> the jury. Hardly ever is a capital case tried in this state but what
> some of the government officers have been witnesses for the
> prosecution, and also had more or less to do in caring for the
> jury.

While Train's assertion was true, it wasn't nearly as compelling as his
previous arguments had been. For example, during the change of
venue debate Train easily cited cases that pertained to the point he was
making. In this instance, he chose not to reference another case (or
couldn't) where said government witness actually bunked with the jury.

He finished by reminding the justices that both motive and premeditation had been established, as proved by the guilty verdict of the
reasonable jury. He could think of no reason to waste the Commonwealth's time and energy with another trial. His own body language
suggested that Train felt his time and energy was being wasted having
to revisit Frost's case at that particular moment.

Now it was up to Colt and Devens. They "briefly considered
the points that had been raised," as *The Worcester West Chronicle* put
it, and then they denied the motion. Colt addressed each of Hopkins'
four claims individually. First, there was no case made to reject the
jury's verdict. Second, Hopkins hadn't shown that Bothwell had inter-
fered with the jury, nor had he proven that the sheriff had been derelict
in his duties while watching over them. Third, Colt agreed with Train
that the sheriff's eating and sleeping with the jury was not overly un-

usual. And fourth, the newspaper issue had been addressed at the time of the trial, and it too was handled properly.

With the decision made, *Commonwealth v. Samuel J. Frost* was officially closed. There would not be a new trial, and there were no other legal avenues of appeal left for Hopkins. Frost got the news in his cell the next day, as reported by *The Worcester Daily Spy*:

> Yesterday morning Sheriff Sprague notified Frost, the Peter-sham murderer, of the decision of the Supreme Court on his petition for another trial, which was heard in Boston Saturday. When informed that the motion had been denied, Frost main-tained the same stolid demeanor which has characterized his conduct since he was first arrested, last August, and did not appear to be affected in the least.

Frost's only hope of avoiding the gallows at that point was an act of clemency by the Governor of the Commonwealth. Unfortunately for him, the timing of his case could not have been worse in that regard.

Prior to 1920, the position of Governor in Massachusetts was filled on a yearly basis. Every November a gubernatorial election was held and the next year's governor was chosen. Men could run for re-election and often did, but they had to face the voters yearly. At the time Frost killed his brother-in-law, William Gatson was serving his first term as Governor. Gatson was a reform Democrat who had previously been the Mayor of Boston, and he was considered to be not nearly as hard line as the previous Republican governors who had preceded him. If Frost had any chance for clemency, Governor Gatson was his man. But Gatson had a major problem in 1875, and it came in the form of a fifteen-year-old boy named Jesse Pomeroy.

Pomeroy was a murderer who had previously garnered even more national attention than Frost did. He'd been tried and convicted of killing ten-year-old Katie Curran of South Boston in December of 1874. During his trial facts came out that proved he had killed at least one other boy (a four-year-old, whom he decapitated), and he had physically tortured many other children in his neighborhood. Despite his age and a recommendation of leniency from his jury (because of his age), Pomeroy was given the death penalty. All that stood between the young killer and the gallows was Governor William Gatson.

Because Pomeroy was so young, his case had been widely argued from the moment of his arrest. Following his sentence, Jesse's lawyer appealed to the Governor's Executive Council, begging them to recommend clemency for his young client. However, twice in 1875 the Executive Council voted AGAINST clemency. In spite of those votes, Governor Gatson refused to sign Jesse's death warrant. *The Boston Post*, among others, had argued vociferously for Gatson to sign the death warrant, and they were not pleased with his failure to do so. Then in November of 1875, Gatson became a one-term Governor, as he was voted out of office in large part due to the uproar caused by his very unpopular decision in the Pomeroy case.

The new Governor in 1876 was a man named Alexander Rice. Like Gatson, Rice had previously been the Mayor of Boston, and he had also been a United States Representative in Congress. But unlike Gatson, he was a conservative Republican, which was not good news for Frost. When Frost's case arrived on his desk, Governor Rice had already asked his Executive Council for a recommendation on the Pomeroy case. While then Governor Gatson had refused to sign Pomeroy's death warrant, he hadn't issue any clemency in the case either, so Rice still had the ability to have Pomeroy executed if he chose. Shockingly, Rice's council recommended clemency for Pomeroy in July of 1876, and Governor Rice followed their recommendation and granted it. (Pomeroy would spend the next forty years in solitary confinement.) But while the Pomeroy case was pending, Rice had two other death warrants to consider — Thomas Piper's and Samuel J. Frost's. Neither man was fifteen, and both had committed heinous acts during their crimes. Piper had raped and murdered four girls, all of whom were under the age of ten. Frost had killed his own brother-in-law and then butchered the corpse. Knowing that he might grant clemency to Pomeroy, which would come with a political cost, Rice was even less likely to consider clemency for Frost and Piper. In fact, signing those two execution warrants might actually buy him some political capital that would help assuage Pomeroy's clemency if he decided to grant it. Thus, almost as soon as the death warrants for the two men arrived on his desk, he signed them. He also set May 26th as the date for both executions, which was well before he would rule on the Pomeroy case.

Once again it fell to Sheriff Sprague to notify Frost of Governor Rice's decision, as told in *The Worcester Daily Spy*:

> The sheriff informed Frost that he had not yet received the governor's warrant, but the action of his excellency had been published in the newspapers, and the official document would

doubtless be received in a day or two. The doomed man heard the announcement sealing his fate with the same stolid, indifferent manner which has characterized his manner ever since his arrest. At first, he said not a word, but seemed to wonder if the information he had received was correct. Sheriff Sprague again repeated his offer to furnish spiritual consolation to Frost, and said that three or four clergymen had expressed a willingness to visit him if he so desired. Frost curtly replied that when he wanted to see anyone he would let him know. He wanted to know what the papers said about his execution, and was furnished with a copy of a paper so that he might himself read what was said.

The Boston Post printed that Frost had been playing a game of checkers with a guard when Sprague delivered the news, but it noted that, "he did not finish the game he was playing when the Sheriff made his announcement." Samuel may have remained "stolid" on the outside, but he knew full well what Sprague's news meant. The checkers game may not have been finished, but he now was.

A week later Hopkins and Ball paid a visit to Samuel in his cell. Hopkins confirmed what Sprague had already said, that things were now beyond hopeless. He dejectedly added that he had reached out to government officials for help, but that none was forthcoming. *The Worcester Daily Spy* noted that Hopkins then told Samuel, "it would be useless to ask the Governor for a commutation." Ever stoic, Frost listened quietly and then thanked his attorneys for all they'd done for him. He then added that, "he hoped they would call and see him often as long as he lives." The two men smiled and nodded affirmatively, and as they were leaving the cell, Ball put his hand on Frost's shoulder and asked him how he was holding up. Frost's reply was quoted in *The Boston Post*, "I haven't as yet shed any tears." His execution was less than a month away.

BOSTON POST.

FRIDAY MORNING, MAY 26, 1876.

ABOUT-HOME MATTERS.

THE GALLOWS.

The Final Preparations for the Execution of Piper and Frost—Their Last Night upon Earth—Brief Recapitulation of their Crimes, Etc.

[REPORTED FOR THE BOSTON POST.]

To-day Thomas W. Piper, the author of the belfry horror, and Samuel J. Frost, the murderer of Franklin B. Towne, his brother-in law, will forfeit their lives on the gallows in expiation of their appalling crimes. In the case of the first-named criminal the feeling throughout the community is one of intense indignation, and but few sympathize with the unfortunate man. The deed for which he dies this morning is one of thrilling horror, and the details the most shocking and revolting that have ever been recorded in the criminal history of this country. The particulars of the dreadful tragedy enacted by Piper, under the very roof of the temple of God, on a bright Sunday afternoon, one year ago, and as told by himself, are yet fresh in the public mind, and therefore a brief recapitulation of this and the other crimes which he claims to have committed is all that will now be necessary.

Page 3 of the *Boston Post* on the morning of Frost's execution
(Courtesy of newspapers.com)

16

The Last Days

The day Samuel J. Frost was arrested, his wife Carrie visited him at the Barre jail. It wasn't so much a visit as it was Carrie dropping off a change of clothes for her husband, per request of Sheriff Bothwell. The only other time the two had seen each other since August 1st was at the trial, and the two obviously did not speak then. And Samuel had not seen his four children at all since the morning of his arrest. As the day of his execution drew near, it appeared he was never going to see any of them again. *The Spy* noted on April 24th that Frost "had no desire to see his wife." That same day *The Springfield Republican* reported:

> Frost hasn't been told yet the day for his execution is fixed. Meanwhile his wife is said to be generally perturbed in mind, and unable to sleep for fear that he will in some way accomplish his threatened revenge.

If those items were accurate, then Frost was still angry with Carrie and Carrie was in fear of Samuel. Any thought that the two would ever lay eyes on each other again before Frost was marched to the gallows seemed unlikely.

But from the time they were married back in 1866, Samuel and Carrie's relationship had been complicated, and that would continue right up until his death. There was no doubt that Carrie had played a critical role in sending the man she affectionately called "J" to the scaffold, and there was also no doubt that Samuel was quite angry about that. In early May, just weeks prior to his death, *The Worcester Daily Spy* reported on another conversation Frost had with his attorneys:

> He entertains a very bitter feeling towards his wife, who he thinks, might have helped him a great deal at the trial without sacrificing anything for the sake of the truth. She could have told things in his favor that would have placed him in a much better light before the jury.

Despite that ill feeling however, Samuel had repeatedly requested that Carrie come to visit him throughout his incarceration. Remember, *The Athol Transcript* of August 31st had this wonderful item tucked
in its 'Local News' column:

> Frost, the murderer, milk spiller, mutilator, and practical sexton
> and resurrectionist, has written his wife, requesting her to come
> and see him, and bring the children, some huckleberries, and
> some clean clothes. She failed to respond. The love and esteem
> that once stood at the flood for him, has silently ebbed and
> ceased forever.

Naturally Samuel wanted to see her *before* the trial, as he was hoping
to influence her testimony. (And maybe get those huckleberries!) But
just days *after* the trial, Frost's two sisters wrote to Carrie begging her
to visit their brother in prison. They also offered to help care for two of
the children if Carrie was now overwhelmed, and they pledged financial support to Carrie if she was in need. Carrie never responded to
them, according to *The Transcript*, as she continued to show no willingness to have anything to do with Samuel or his family.

Then in early May, as their brother's execution neared, those
same sisters visited Samuel in prison. As *The Boston Post* noted:

> The interview is described as having been a very affecting one
> as far as they were concerned, and they were much overcome by
> the thought of the impending fate of their brother. The inter-
> view mainly related to the wife of Frost, and an effort is to be
> made to induce Mrs. Frost with the children to visit him before
> the execution, though she has thus far stoutly refused to do so.

Although Samuel had "no desire to see his wife" in late April, he'd apparently had a change of heart in early May.

The sisters' persistence paid off, as this time they were not
ignored by Carrie. Whatever they said caused her to relent, and on
May 11th she and the children made the trip to Worcester to see Samuel. Thus, the woman who had supposedly stated that she "wished her
husband hung", the woman who'd steadfastly refused to meet with his
attorneys, the woman who'd never brought Samuel any huckleberries...
that same woman finally decided to see her "J." And she'd brought the
children too. *The Boston Globe* reported on the visit two days later:

The Petersham murderer, Frost, held the final interview with
his wife and children Thursday afternoon. The interview from
its nature is not public property, as far as details are concerned,
and there were no statements made or confessions which would
be of public interest. Frost received and parted with the family
in a calm manner and perhaps with as much affection and regard as was to be expected from one who has shown his dispo-
sition… The children are all young and cannot fully realize the
position in which they were placed, and over their meeting with
their father a veil should be drawn.

The story painted a predictably sad picture, and from it one could easily
surmise that Carrie only agreed to the meeting for the sake of the children. However, that turned out not to be the case, as the *Globe* story
continued:

Mrs. Frost, who had previously once seen her husband, showed
a deep sympathy for him and acted in all her conversation the
part of a true, devoted wife, as the condemned man has said,
since his conviction, she was up to the time of the murder. Mrs.
Frost, in her interview with her husband, has showed that she
acted at the trial merely from conscientious duty and not because she had not regard and feeling for the unfortunate man.

Was Carrie merely acting the part for Samuel's benefit? Might *The
Boston Globe* have embellished the story for the sake of its readers? Or
was Carrie genuinely moved after seeing the man she once loved face
to face for the first time in six months? It turned out to be the latter.
In fact, two weeks later — just two days before Samuel was to climb
the scaffold — Carrie visited him again, this time without the children.
The Worcester Daily Spy included this one sentence in a story predomi-
nantly about the preparations being made for the pending execution:

Yesterday afternoon Mrs. Frost visited her husband for the last
time, with Sheriff Sprague alone being present with them in the
corridor.

This was the only sentence ever written about that visit. If Carrie
hugged or kissed her husband in that corridor, Sprague never said. Nor
did he speak to what the couple's last words were to each other. But the

visit made one thing clear. While Samuel was trying his best to remain hard to the end, Carrie was not. She had finally softened, and in so doing she evinced genuine feelings for the man who had murdered her brother. Theirs was indeed a complicated relationship.

That last visit with Carrie on May 24th must have been difficult for Samuel. May 25th would prove to be no easier. The day before his execution began with one last visit by Reverend Lamson, who would walk with Samuel up to the gallows the next day. The two men had come to understand each other over the last few weeks, and this encounter was emblematic of their relationship. Frost thanked Lamson for his many recent visits, Lamson offered his spiritual services one last time (Frost again declined), and then the two men chatted about other topics as they always did. It was a strange coupling to be sure. Lamson of course knew that Frost was a murderer, and Frost had little interest in Lamson's business. Yet the two men had somehow bonded in spite of those issues. And as the reverend exited his cell that morning, Samuel felt a certain twinge of sadness knowing this was the last such meeting between the two.

Not long after Lamson departed, Sheriff Sprague, who was busy making sure everything was in order for the next day's event, informed his prisoner that he had other visitors. One of Frost's sisters had come to pay him a final visit, and she was not alone. Samuel's *mother* had also decided to see her son on the eve of his execution. As *The Worcester Daily Spy* noted, the visit "was quite unexpected, and the scene was quite affecting."

Beginning with the very first reports of the case, not one word had been written about Frost's mother. There had been no mention of her having attended the trial or of her ever having visited Samuel in prison. Nor was there any indication that she'd written to him at any point throughout the entire ordeal. Presumably the last time she'd seen him was the year prior when Samuel visited the mysterious Mr. Whitehouse up in New Hampshire. Rachel Frost was 65 years old, she had raised seven children (Samuel was the second oldest), and she had been widowed some fifteen years earlier. Her daughters had surely kept her abreast of the goings on involving her son, but she had stayed away from it all, until now.

Unfortunately, nothing other than that one line in *The Spy* was ever written about her visit. Sheriff Sprague had been quite liberal in sharing the details of Frost's prison life with the press, but he was silent on both Carrie's and Rachel's last visits. Samuel had vowed to "die game," and he had told Lamson many times that he "wasn't afraid to meet God." Stolid indifference had long been the order of business for Samuel. Unexpectedly seeing his mother on the eve of his execution however, *that* had to have shaken him. But if indeed it did, neither the sheriff nor Rachel ever said.

Sprague did however provide the press with a detailed account of the prisoner's last hours following his mother's visit. Samuel went to bed some time after 7:00pm, and by Sprague's account Frost slept soundly. When he awoke on the morning of the 26th he began to dress, as was his routine. Special Officer Cleveland, one of the men charged with keeping 24-hour watch over Frost, said to him, "You've got the most nerve I ever saw." Frost's response was, "I'm not afraid. I've never been afraid to die." Then as he buttoned up his shirt he boasted:

I'm the happiest man in the prison this morning.

His last meal consisted of brown bread (his favorite), a chunk of cheese, and a cup of milk, which he devoured by 6:00am. His appetite on this morning was in stark contrast to the one on the morning of July 4th, when "he didn't eat much" of his breakfast then, as he himself testified. (Apparently Frank's death bothered him much more than his own.) After he'd finished eating, Frost was moved out of his cell in the west wing of the prison and transferred to the north wing. As *The Worcester Daily Spy* pointed out, he was "passed through the kitchen instead of the guard room" to get there. The Guard Room was the more direct route, but it now contained a scaffold that Sprague did not want Samuel to see, so through the kitchen he went.

Sheriff Bothwell, Deputy Earle, and Deputy Keene, along with several other guards, were waiting at Frost's new holding cell. Samuel inquired as to what had been written about him in the papers (Sprague had begun cutting out all references to the execution from the newspapers he gave Frost), and he also asked about Thomas Piper's pending execution in Boston. Then at 8:00am Reverend Lamson arrived, as did Hopkins, Ball, and the husband of one of Frost's sisters.

Once everyone was situated, Frost began dictating a series of letters to Reverend Lamson. The first was a statement to be given to the press following his hanging. This is how it appeared in *The Worcester Daily Spy* the next day:

After speaking of the killing of Towne, he said: I placed his limbs as I have affirmed in the cornfield. I did not know, neither do I know, who removed them. I took them from under the barn with my own hands to the cornfield, and never carried them to the swamp. On the night of the 22nd of July I did not take the oxen from the barn, nor on any other night, to draw the body to the swamp. I make the same statement as to the whole matter that Mr. Ball has in his book (this refers to Frost's statement at the trial); I declare to all men that I die innocent of willful murder. I die cherishing no feeling of resentment towards anyone. I die forgiving all the world for any wrong I have received. It is hard, but I freely do it. I desire to express my kindest feelings to Gen. Sprague, his deputies, and all the prison officers. To his counsel he said, "Try and keep track of this matter; I hope that in time and am assured that it will be cleared up; I feel that in six months men will say, 'If we hadn't hung that man, we shouldn't.'"

Frost had remained strident until the end. His statement offered no apologies, nor did it seek forgiveness. But in a strange twist, Frost did forgive those who had wronged him! And he was still claiming he never meant to kill Frank Towne. Had he had it to do over, Frost might well have said all of this to the jury before it began deliberations, instead of saying, "I leave it to my counsel."

Next, he dictated letters to his children. It is not known exactly what they said, but they appear to have been what one would expect, at least according to *The Athol Transcript*:

Those to his children were of advice and direction for their conduct in their future lives, and expressing his feeling of sadness at the manner of his parting with them and with life.

Finally, he dictated one last letter for Carrie. What happened then is a matter of some dispute. *The Worcester Daily Spy* merely noted that he wrote letters to his wife and children and reported nothing further about it. *The Athol Transcript* on the other hand, reported the following:

His letter to his wife began in his usual tone, severe and vindictive, but right in the middle of it Frost broke entirely down, holding his head with his arms, and sobbing violently. These were the first tears which he is known to have shed, since his incarceration. After recovering self-control he resumed the dictation of the letter, changing its whole tone and character. The man in him had at last obtained the ascendancy, and he dictated in direct terms his kindly feeling and sympathy for his wife in what she had to suffer, and his free forgiveness for any wrong which he thought she might have done him.

Did Samuel really break down and sob "violently"? *The Transcript* was the only paper to report that he did, and it would have been highly irregular for the Worcester papers not to print it if they'd heard the same story. Further, at the time he dictated Carrie's letter there were at least a dozen men in and around Frost's cell. For a man who's stated goal was to remain tough until the end, the last thing he would have wanted to do was break down in front of all those witnesses. Plus, he'd already said his personal goodbye to Carrie the day before. It would seem much more likely that he would have sobbed in private with her then when he dictated the letter to her surrounded by all those men.

Regardless, when he'd finished Carrie's letter, he was told it was time to change into the black suit he would wear up to the gallows. As he did so, he asked Reverend Lamson for one final favor. It turned out that at some point during the week Samuel *had allowed his photograph to be taken* for the first and only time in his life. He gave the resulting three photos to Lamson, along with the names of the three people to whom he wanted those photos to be given. (Carrie? His mother? One of his sisters?) He then made Lamson promise that no one but those three would ever get those photos. Lamson gave Samuel his word.

And then it was time. One by one the men trickled out of Frost's cell to take their places either in the procession or in the Guard Room. Frost was escorted into the hallway and positioned amongst the deputies. Sheriff Sprague whispered something to him, and Frost gently nodded. Finally, after the men stood there quietly for a moment, Sprague checked his watch and then made his way into the Guard Room. Samuel J. Frost's execution was about to begin.

Sheriff Augustus B. R. Sprague
(As printed in *The Worcester Magazine* in June 1910)

17

The Fallout

Frost's execution was only the thirteenth in the history of Worcester County and it was the first in eight years. Eyes were on it and it had gone horribly wrong. As such, there were going to be questions asked and fingers pointed. The day after Frost's head was almost ripped completely off of his body, *The Fitchburg Sentinel* began its lengthy editorial on the matter with this plea:

> It ought to be true that Massachusetts, Friday, made a long stride toward the abolition of capital punishment. The spectacular drama in the jail at Worcester ought to have afforded ghastly horror enough to last a generation at least.

The Springfield Republican's May 27th edition offered this:

> Curious how blood shocks some people who are not shocked at all at the idea of taking a man's life. Is there any way of insurance against making a mess of it? Even the professional hand couldn't guarantee the strength of a man's neck. Ghastly? Well, whose fault is it, unless it be of those who demand life for life? Even the state cannot make murder a fine art, and she better cease experimenting.

Even the pro-death penalty *The Boston Post* (the very paper that six months earlier had helped run Governor Gatson out of office) felt the need to express some concern over what had taken place:

> The public sense of justice is satisfied, and society not only feels vindicated, but breathes more freely now that the extreme penalty of the law has been carried out. But whether hanging is the most decorous method of inflicting the death penalty may be questioned after the experience of the scene at Worcester.

Frost's botched hanging was the talk of the Commonwealth, and for all the wrong reasons. And while the newspaper accounts of the scene were bad enough, the twisted versions that were being told in every bar and on every street corner had people's eyes open wide in disbelief.

There was one man who didn't need to read the newspapers or walk into a bar to know he had a problem. Sheriff Sprague knew it the second he heard the crowd gasp after he had stepped on "the drop." Nonetheless, he *had* read the newspapers the next day just like everyone else (nobody had cut out the references to the execution for him as he had done for Frost), and he knew he had to do something. Two days later, when people picked up *The Worcester Daily Spy* on Monday the 29th, they found out what that something was. The sheriff had written a letter to the paper, stating categorically that he was not going to let Frost's bungled execution get pinned on him:

> Editor Spy: I have shrunk from making any public statement in regard to the performance of an unpleasant official duty on Friday last, till continued exaggeration and misrepresentation in some of the newspapers, whose correspondents were present by my courtesy, compel me, if not in my own defense, at least in defense of my assistants, to state a few facts which cannot be controverted.
>
> The scaffold was of the same height, floor-trap and beam, the rope and noose precisely like the one used at the same hour at the Boston jail for the execution of Piper.
>
> The fall of Frost was at least six inches less than Piper. The noose was adjusted in the same manner, the knot at the same place on the neck, of the same tension as nearly as possible, as that successfully used at the last three executions which took place at Boston.
>
> The adjustment of the straps, cap and noose was made by a cool, intelligent and thoroughly competent officer, as all who know Deputy Sheriff D. M. Earle will unhesitatingly aver.
>
> Each officer performed his part without hesitation, without undue haste, and without blunder, and I cannot conceive how human foresight could have anticipated anything but a successful issue.
>
> In light of my experience I could suggest no alteration or improvement in the preparations should it become my misfortune to again perform this official duty.

The head was *not* "severed from the body," as announced on bulletin-boards and in the papers. The rope was *not* improperly adjusted and did *not* cut into the neck, but the separation took place at a point below the cord.

I protest against the use of such terms as "barbaric spectacle" and "sickening sight," with reference to this occurrence, to create a sensation, when the opinions of distinguished physicians present were freely given at the time that death was instantaneous; or any criticism upon my acts of courtesy, or apology for anything done or left undone by myself or my assistants, clearly conscious of having performed a sad duty humanely and with all possible precaution to prevent prolonged mental or physical suffering on the part of the unfortunate criminal.

A.B.R. Sprague,
Sheriff of Worcester County.
Saturday evening, May 27.

Normally such a public comment would have been highly irregular, but Sprague had little choice in this case. Prolonged silence from him would have only led to more accusations. And based on the defensive tone of his note, it was clear that he'd heard all sorts of rumor and speculation about the incident. Augustus B.R. Sprague was not the sort of man to let such scandalous hearsay go unchecked. While his note's tone was defensive, its message was aggressive. Sprague and his men had done their jobs to the best of their abilities, and they had done everything by the book. Further, the preparations made and the scaffold used were exactly the same as those in the Piper execution held in Boston that same day, and that execution had gone flawlessly. (They'd even used the same rope!) No one could reasonably explain why one had succeeded while the other had failed. The sheriff, to his credit, wasn't pointing fingers at anyone, but his letter made clear that no fingers were to be pointed at him either. Yes something had gone wrong, but no one in his department was to blame for that.

As is often the case with such public outcries, things calmed down quickly after the initial shock wore off. As a matter of fact, on the very day Sprague's letter ran, that same *Worcester Daily Spy* also printed a notice announcing that the sheriff would be the Guest of Honor in the Memorial Day parade in Grafton. Sprague had long been a highly respected man in Worcester County, and what happened with Samuel J. Frost was not going to change that. Yes, people were momentarily outraged over what had happened, but they liked and trusted their sheriff. As proof of that, *The Fitchburg Sentinel* published an editorial in its evening edition on the 27th, which said in part:

> Some of the morning papers, as well as private individuals, have made remarks upon the officers in charge of the execution of Samuel J. Frost at Worcester, inferring that the accident which made the execution appalling to observers might have been prevented… Too much praise cannot be bestowed upon Sheriff Sprague for his humane treatment of his prisoner, Samuel J. Frost, both before and at the time of his execution. Death was painless as well as instantaneous.

The storm had come hard and fast for Sheriff Sprague, but it passed just as quickly. His letter had in large measure seen to that. There were no calls for his resignation, there were no public investigations, and once everybody had read Sprague's letter, there was no need for further explanations.

There were also no more executions, not in Worcester County anyway. It was very much to Sprague's benefit that it never did "become his misfortune to again perform this official duty." Sprague remained sheriff until 1890, but whether by happenstance or design, no prisoner was sentenced to death in Worcester County during that time. As a result, Sprague never had to answer public questions about Frost's execution again, and he never had to read any quips such as these in any local newspaper — *let us hope this execution goes better than the last one*, or *it appears that Worcester County believes in the mantra 'if at first you don't succeed, try, try again.'* A subsequent hanging certainly would have forced Sprague to revisit Frost's, but fortunately for him that never happened.

With that said, there were plenty more executions by hanging in Massachusetts. Lest anyone think that the Frost spectacle spurred a statewide movement to do away with public hangings, it did not. Had the roles on May 26th, 1876, been reversed, and had it been the Piper execution in Boston that had gone horribly wrong, things *might* have changed. Had Governor Gaston signed Jesse Pomeroy's death warrant and had the "boy murderer" been nearly decapitated under the scaffold, things *definitely* would have changed. But for most people, especially those in Boston, Worcester County was out of sight and quickly out of mind. There simply wasn't going to be any sea change brought on by what had happened to a 41-year-old farmer from Petersham who'd killed his brother-in-law.

The next such execution in Boston occurred three years later in 1879. Two years prior, William Devlin had returned to his Lowell home after a night of hard drinking, and he quickly got into a shouting match with his wife. When she finally admitted to having borrowed a quarter from a friend in order to pay for a tooth to be extracted (her "crime" was that she hadn't first sought his permission to borrow the money), Devlin spun into a drunken rage and beat her mercilessly until he killed her. For his actions Devlin was given the death penalty, which the Commonwealth carried out on March 14th, 1879, in Cambridge (just outside of Boston). Buried deep inside *The Boston Post's* lengthy description of Devlin's execution the next day was one very ironic line:

> At twenty minutes past ten, the visitors, with the exception of Father O'Donnell, withdrew, and while the dying litany was being said, Sheriffs Sprague of Worcester and Herrick of Essex, with Capt. Adams, made a careful inspection of the gallows.

It had been less than three years since Frost's hanging had gone so wrong, and yet there was Sheriff Sprague making sure the gallows were properly assembled for Devlin! Sprague's participation that day made it clear that what had happened to Samuel J. Frost hadn't tarnished the sheriff in the slightest.

In all, Massachusetts carried out fourteen more hangings by the end of the century, none in Worcester County. Beginning in 1900, the Commonwealth changed its means of carrying out a death sentence from hanging to the electric chair. When the change was made, the state also decided to place "Old Sparky" only in state prisons, not in county jails. Thus, of the sixty-six electric chair executions carried out before Massachusetts did away with the death penalty in 1948, none were done in the "Middle District." As such, Samuel J. Frost was not only the last man to be hanged in Worcester County, he was also the last man ever executed in Worcester County.

WORCESTER COUNTY.

It wouldn't do to submit the Worcester newspaper men to the ordeal of a Frost hanging, every day. One of them sagely observes: "In connection with the awful punishments dealt to the murderers, Piper and Frost, yesterday, many persons in the city noticed an ominous appearance in the heavens during the afternoon. It was nothing more than a star visible to the naked eye in bright midday, and situated in close proximity and to the southwest of the plainly outlined figure of the new moon,"—all of which is somehow very dreadful and mysterious, and terribly unsettling to the poor fellow's nerves.

The last mention of Samuel J. Frost in *The Springfield Republican* on May 29, 1876.

Postscript

Thus endeth the story of one Samuel J. Frost, the Petersham Butcher of 1875.

BUT...

There is one thing that needs to be cleared up before this book is finished: he never said it. HE NEVER SAID IT! Samuel J. Frost never said those eight words that first brought his name to the attention of a snot-nosed little kid in Petersham more than a hundred years after his death. He never said, "There will be a Frost in Hell tonight."

Frost's last days were well documented in the local papers. His spoken words were quoted extensively, and his written statement was published verbatim. He certainly did utter some memorable lines in his last few hours. For starters, he proclaimed, "I'm the happiest man in the prison this morning" on the day of his execution. His written statement ended with the prognostication, "I feel that in six months men will say, 'If we hadn't hung him, we shouldn't.'" (It turns out he was no better at predicting his future than he was at concealing his past — no one ever said that.) That statement also included the strange lines, "I die forgiving all the world for what wrong I have received. It is hard, but I freely do it." (The public was looking for contrition, instead they got Frost's indignation.) And lest we forget, he also told that incredulous prison guard, "I've never been afraid to die." The reality is that Samuel J. Frost turned a number of memorable phrases as his death approached; he just didn't turn *that memorable phrase*. Had he, there is no doubt that newspapers across the country would have printed it. "Frost Indeed in Hell" very likely would have been the headline in place of the various "ghastly" and "horrible" versions that were used. Instead, that famous line is nowhere to be found in print back in 1876.

So the question is, if Samuel J. Frost didn't say it, who did? Well, as with most local legends, no one knows for sure. Stories in small New England towns get embellished at community picnics, church socials, county fairs, etc. (Not to mention at the local watering holes!) As those stories get passed down, they get more and more colorful while often becoming less and less factual. Consequently, who first affixed that memorable quote to Frost's story and when exactly it was added will never be known for certain.

However, while the quote's origin remains a mystery, the genesis of its becoming "fact" does not. In 1948 the fabled Petersham historian Mabel Coolidge published her definitive book, *The History of Petersham, Massachusetts, Incorporated April 20, 1754*. It was a massive tome, detailing anything and everything that ever happened in the Hilltop Town. Buried deep inside that book, hidden amongst a group of funny quotes relating to Petersham, is the following found on page 258:

> When Samuel J. Frost was to be executed, May 26, 1876, the jailer remarked, "It is a warm sunny morning." To which the victim replied, "Yes, but there will be a Frost in Hell tonight."

Either Mabel had a better source in 1948 than the newspapers did in 1876, or she simply couldn't resist including such a fantastic quote, regardless of its veracity. And who could blame her really, it is a fantastic quote. But the story does bring to mind a baseball hat that was once sold in the Country Store, the front of which bore a slogan explaining how to properly pronounce the town's name. It proudly declared, "There's no 'sham' in Petersham!" While that's true, there was one little innocent 'sham' in *The History of Petersham*.

Nonetheless, I will forever be indebted to Mabel for printing that anecdote, for without those eight words I would have never wondered about "a man named Frost." Had I not been made aware of Frost's apocryphal phrase, I might well be staring at a computer screen right now, wondering how to tell the story of Calvin Coolidge and his fishing buddy. Faced with that arduous task, I'd probably be making up Cal's "first words," just as Mabel made up Frost's "last words." And while it may indeed be true that Frost is down in Hell while Mabel surely sits comfortably up in Heaven, I'm guessing both of them have big grins on their faces knowing that those eight fictitious words will forever be a part of the true history of the little town I grew up in, a place you'd never heard of before . . . Petersham, Massachusetts.

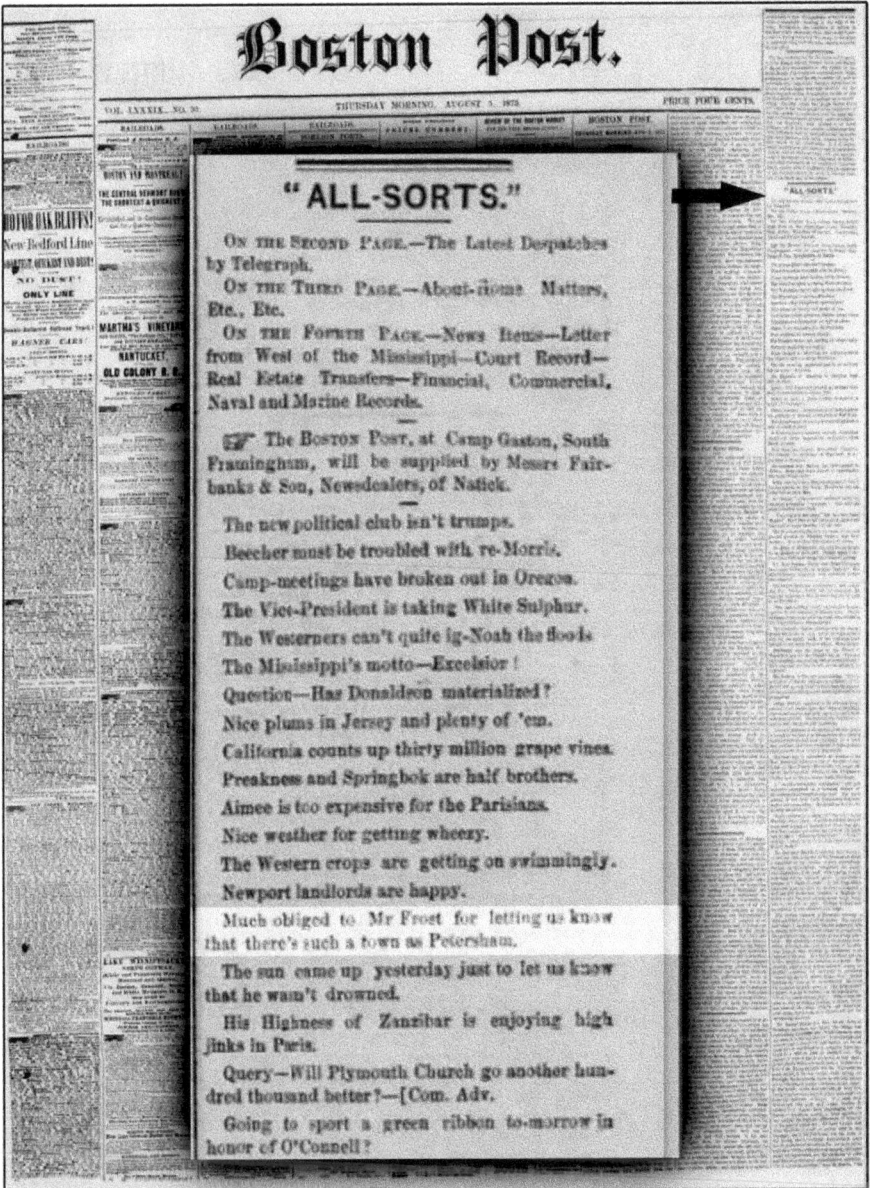

"ALL-SORTS."

ON THE SECOND PAGE.—The Latest Despatches by Telegraph.

ON THE THIRD PAGE.—About-Home Matters, Etc., Etc.

ON THE FOURTH PAGE.—News Items—Letter from West of the Mississippi—Court Record—Real Estate Transfers—Financial, Commercial, Naval and Marine Records.

The BOSTON POST, at Camp Gaston, South Framingham, will be supplied by Messrs Fairbanks & Son, Newsdealers, of Natick.

The new political club isn't trumps.

Beecher must be troubled with re-Morris.

Camp-meetings have broken out in Oregon.

The Vice-President is taking White Sulphur.

The Westerners can't quite ig-Noah the floods.

The Mississippi's motto—Excelsior!

Question—Has Donaldson materialized?

Nice plums in Jersey and plenty of 'em.

California counts up thirty million grape vines.

Preakness and Springbok are half brothers.

Aimee is too expensive for the Parisians.

Nice weather for getting wheezy.

The Western crops are getting on swimmingly.

Newport landlords are happy.

Much obliged to Mr Frost for letting us know that there's such a town as Petersham.

The sun came up yesterday just to let us know that he wasn't drowned.

His Highness of Zanzibar is enjoying high jinks in Paris.

Query—Will Plymouth Church go another hundred thousand better?—[Com. Adv.

Going to sport a green ribbon to-morrow in honor of O'Connell?

The *Boston Post of August 5, 1875*
(Courtesy of newspapers.com)

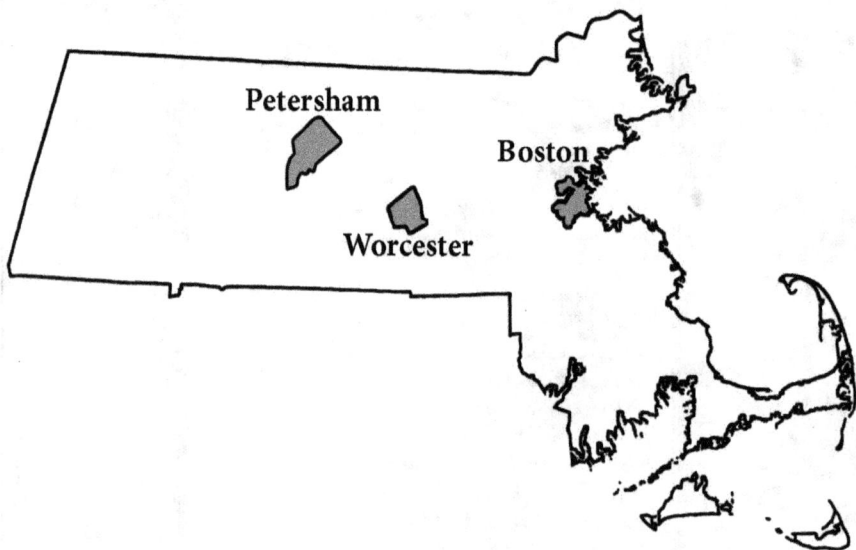

"This was assuredly a 'murder most foul.'
Its like seldom stains the record of Massachusetts."

The Athol Transcript - August 10, 1875

Frank Towne's gravestone
(Nichewaug Cemetery in Petersham, MA)

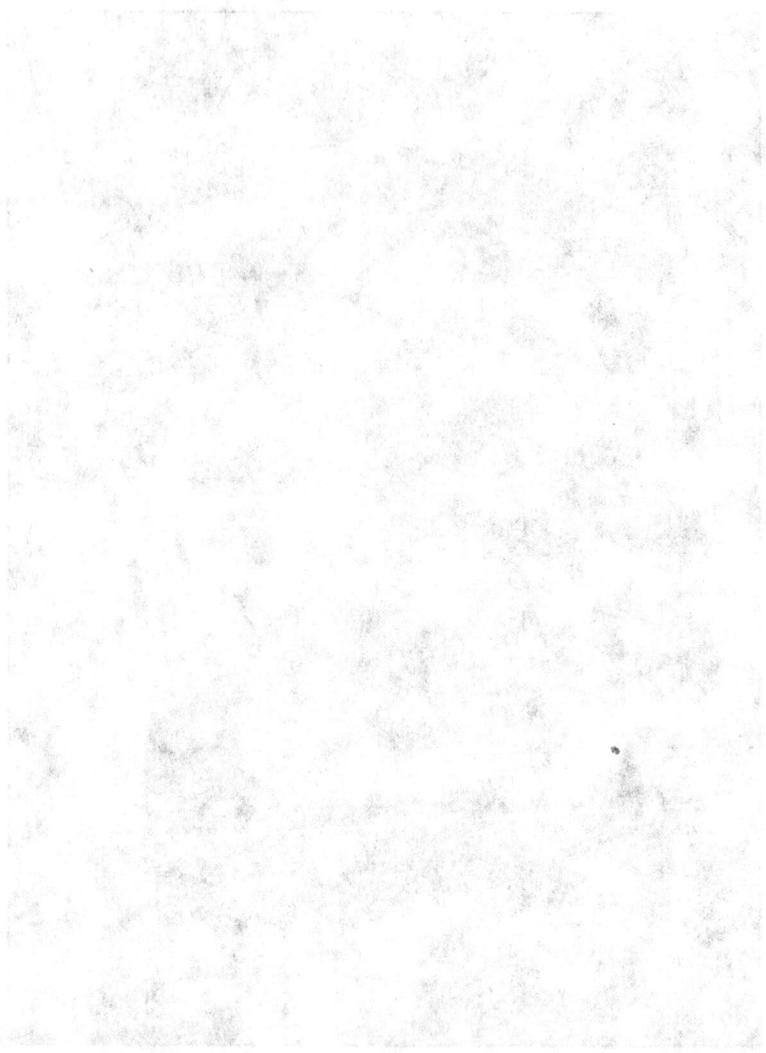

Acknowledgements

There are so many people to thank for helping make this book possible. Let me start with three ladies who went above and beyond in helping me. First and foremost, I owe a special debt of gratitude to Linda Libert, who graciously and painstakingly edited this book. I now know why so many writers have a love/hate relationship with their editors, as there were many times when I cursed Linda out late at night after she'd sent me back a chapter that she'd completely gutted. And yes Linda, I still can't believe you made me take out the phrase, "this wasn't his first rodeo!" (She said it didn't fit the 1875 time frame, which I will admit is technically true.) That said, I'm also sure that when she reads this book again, she will be cursing me out as she notices I didn't follow *every* suggested edit she recommended! But in spite of all that, this book is infinitely better as a result of her efforts, and I am forever grateful Linda, thank you.

Then there's Darlene Wildes of the Westminster Historical Society. Darlene and I had many correspondences about Eli Merriam, one of the men who served on Frost's jury. At long last, Darlene was able to track down Eli's picture for me. There can be no doubt that she too is cursing me now, having realized I never ended up using that photo in the book! I'm sorry Darlene, but I thank you for your repeated efforts in helping me research that most interesting man. (She also sent several articles to me about the case - via snail mail! – which were very helpful.)

Finally, Christine Mandel of the Petersham Historical Society endured far too many emails from me, and I'm fairly certain she thought I was never actually going to finish this book! With that said, I couldn't have finished it without her assistance, and I must thank her again for providing so many of the photos that appear in these pages. I must also apologize to Christine for asking over and over again, *"are you sure* you don't have a photo of Joseph W. Upton?" Come to think of it Christine, *"are you sure* you don't have a photo of SAMUEL Upton?!!!"* Thank you Christine!

Not to be outdone, there are three gentlemen I must also thank right upfront, starting with one Gene Lavanchy. Gene has a favorite joke that goes, "a friend will help you move, but a good friend will help you move *a body*." If I can rework that joke just a little, "a friend will buy your book, and a good friend will actually read it, but a *really* good friend will relentlessly harass strangers at book signings until they buy your book." There was a poor lady outside of *Blast From the Past* in Falmouth who had the "audacity" to try and walk by the store while wearing a Nantucket sweatshirt without first checking out my new book *ACK in Ashes*. That idea wasn't working for Gene, who proceeded to "discuss" the matter with her. When she finally walked into the store and bought my book, she had a look of pure abject fear upon her face, and she made sure to show Gene she'd bought a copy on the way out of the store! I'll be counting on much more of that with this book Geno. (I'm thinking maybe a full-sized wooden sandwich board and a megaphone this time around, yes?)

Speaking of good friends, thank you Tom Samoluk. Tom bought *ACK in Ashes* and then told me, "but there's no way I'm ever going to read this. I can't read books. I fall asleep within the first page." But Tom took *ACK* with him on a Caribbean vacation, and yes indeed, he finished the book right there on the beach! I know this because he sent me a beaming selfie, complete with the book and a sunburned chest!!! Some time later while we were at a Red Sox game Tom asked me what my next book was going to be about. I briefly told him about this story, but then I meekly offered that I didn't think I'd ever find the time to write it. He simply said, "Well, it sounds interesting. If you write it, I'll read it. Now let's get some Fenway Franks." I'll be expecting a ballpark selfie with this book Tom, but maybe keep your shirt on this time!

Then there's the other person who shocked me by reading *ACK* — my brother Michael. Fludge, as he is known, is an avid magazine reader (*Pro Football Weekly*, *Rolling Stone*, and *DownEast* come to mind), but not so much with books. In fact, the only two books I know that he's read completely are *Ivanhoe* (he did a book report on that one for 10th, 11th, and 12th grades in high school!) and *No One Here Gets Out Alive*, the book about Jim Morrison and the Doors. However, Fludge was the first of my siblings to read *ACK* cover to cover, and I appreciate that more than he knows. I'm certain he's going to do the same with this book, and call me crazy, but I think he's going to like this one even more than *Ivanhoe*!

When taking on a project like this, one of the many upsides is you get to meet so many good people that you otherwise would never have known. I'll start with the staff at the fantastic American Antiquarian Society. Without access to their *Worcester Daily Spy* collection, this book simply couldn't exist. The same holds true for the Athol Public Library and its *Athol Transcript* collection. Then there's the Social Law Library in Boston; no matter how much time I spend in that place, it will never be enough. The Harvard Historical Society, the Massachusetts Historical Society, the Uxbridge Town Library, the Barre Library... I am indebted to you all. To Mike and Kim Cosco at West Boxford Provisions, who held my first-ever book signing, I'm on my way again, get the table ready! Likewise Steve Rotondi at the Stoneham Historical Society; Steve actually took *ACK* with him on an Alaskan cruise, so I can't wait to see where he takes *Frost*! In addition, random thanks go to fellow historian and popover lover Paul Debole (finish *your* book!), Vanessa Hale (she sat through not one but TWO of my lectures on *ACK*), and Connie Hackenson (I sent her on multiple wild goose chases at the Worcester County Courthouse). You all know why I'm thanking you. A special mention must also be made of Michael McCarron, the Town Clerk in West Newbury, MA. Your patience in finding the Frosts' wedding certificate is greatly appreciated by me, and the candy selection at your desk is greatly appreciated by my four-year-old son Owen!

Then there's Guy Glodis, the former Sheriff of Worcester County. If I didn't acknowledge him he would forever scream at me, "how could you write a book about Worcester County and not mention me?" I once asked him if there was any truth to the rumor that the Sheriff's office had kept the noose used to hang Frost. Sheriff Glodis responded, "Are you out of your mind? We don't have anything like that around here. Smarten up." Sheriff Sprague couldn't have said it better Guy! By the way, if I actually get Glodis to read this book from start to finish I will have accomplished something many thought impossible...

A more serious thank you goes to anyone and everyone who has ever loaded a newspaper that has ended up on newspapers.com. That website is beyond invaluable, and it greatly enriches stories like these. The same goes for the people at ancestry.com, a website I've spent far too much time on recently! Also, anyone who took the time to provide me with feedback on my first book at my website vbthewise.com, I thank you sincerely and hope that you will do the same for this book.

Two more. First, a special thank you to Cocoa, my beautiful wife. She couldn't have been more "excited" when I told her I was going to write this book. She was several months pregnant with our FOURTH child at the time, and the "joy" at my announcement was written all over her face! And that look was nothing compared to the one she gave me a year later when I told her what I was thinking of as an image for the book cover. Her mouth said nothing, but her eyes were screaming, "my God, I've married a moron!" She waved me away silently, and then an hour later she showed me her concept for the book cover. I'm betting you can guess whose concept was better. In between those two "you gotta be kidding me?" moments, on multiple occasions Cocoa took all four of our kids to her mother's so I could have long weekends alone to write. If you knew her mother you'd know just how big a sacrifice that is! (I kid, but Linda did make her fabulous book club read *ACK*, so thank you too mom-in-law.) By the way Cocoa, while I dedicated this book to your brother, you're an early contender for that honor in book #3. Wait, have I not told you yet about book #3? And there's that look again...

Finally, there's Mom. In the spring of 1969 she already had SEVEN kids, and there was another one relaxing comfortably in her belly — me. In need of a bigger house and more space for her little rascals to roam, Mom moved the family away from the south shore of Massachusetts to a town she had absolutely no connection to – Petersham. Three months later, I popped out of her stomach and reportedly said, "This town better have something to offer..." No one knew it then, but this book actually began on that hot summer day. Thanks for making that move Mom, and thanks for EVERYTHING. I love you, and I hope that my writing this book about a diabolical murder and a horrific execution helps prove that!

To all of you, I am truly grateful. Thank you.

Nːtes and Bibliːgraphy

The bulk of this book comes from five main sources. The most important of which is the official trial transcript of *Commonwealth v. Frost*, found at The Social Law Library in Boston. Whenever possible, I tried to let the people involved in the case speak for themselves, and most of that comes from that transcript. For example, the story of Frost having lent his horse to Coroner Shattuck for the ride to the Barre Jail, it was Shattuck himself who testified to that in court. In other instances, there were two very different stories told in court as to what happened, so there were times I had to make judgment calls as to whom to believe. In those cases, I tried my best to use the facts presented at trial and the newspaper reports at the time to piece together who was telling the truth. For example, Frost was adamant right up to his death that he never used his team of oxen to move Towne's body. Carrie was adamant that he did, and there was enough circumstantial evidence to back her up that I sided with her on that point. There was also some dispute as to the spelling of names. George Josselyn's name was spelled multiple different ways in the newspapers at the time. In all cases I tried to use the spelling that seemed to be the most prevalent. Thus, "Josselyn" was used instead of "Joslin" or "Joslyn," and "Rathbone" was used instead of "Rathburn."

The four other critical sources for the book were the following newspapers: *The Worcester Daily Spy*, *The Athol Transcript*, *The Fitchburg Sentinel*, and *The Boston Post*. I chose not to use formal footnotes for this book because they would have quickly gotten repetitive. Instead, I tried to site these papers and the accompanying dates whenever possible in the text. On rare occasion I decided not to cite the papers specifically for flow purposes. For example, in chapter 7 Carrie Frost's description as being a "matronly appearing woman" was from *The Worcester Daily Spy*, while it was *The Fitchburg Daily Sentinel* that noted she was "clad in deep mourning." In general, these newspapers proved invaluable from August 3rd, 1875, to June 1st, 1876. Three other papers also contributed multiple times to filling in the story: *The Boston Globe*,

The Springfield Republican, and *The Worcester West Chronicle*. Again, I dated those references within the text.

The other sources that contributed to this book are as follows:

Shays's Rebellion: The American Revolution's Final Battle, by Leonard Richards. UPenn Press, Philadelphia, PA 2002.

Tornado! 84 Minutes, 94 Lives, by John M. O'Toole. DATABOOKS publishing, Worcester, MA 1993.

Legal Executions in New England: A Comprehensive Reference, 1623-1960, by Daniel Allen Hearn. McFarland and Company Inc., Jefferson, NC, 1999. p. 257 has a profile of the Frost execution.

Reminiscences of Worcester from the Earliest Period, Historical and Genealogical, by Caleb A. Wall. Tyler and Seagrave Publishing, Worcester, MA, 1877. (Contains the story of the James brothers' 1868 execution.)

Murderpedia.org "Jesse Harding Pomeroy."

Gizmodo.com "The Fiendish Life of Jesse Pomeroy, Teen Serial Killer," by John Marr. June 24, 2015.

Historicalcrimedetective.com "Jesse Pomeroy: America's Youngest Serial Killer"

The Public Statutes of the Commonwealth of Massachusetts, Enacted November 19, 1881. Wright and Potter Printing, Boston, MA 1886.

Fortdevensmuseum.org "General Devens Survived War to Become U.S. Attorney General, Judge", by Don Eriksson, September 1, 2004.

Rootsweb.ancestry.com Biography by Kenneth Robinson II

Biographical Encyclopedia of Massachusetts of the Nineteenth Century vol. 2 by H. Clay Williams Metropolitan Publishing, Boston, 1883. Charles Devens profile on p. 102-116.

Biographical Directory of the United States Executive Branch 1774-1989, Robert Sobel editor, Greenwood Press, Westport, CT, 1990. p. 102 has a Devens biography.

Mass.gov "Associate Justice Charles Devens Memorial"

Charles Devens: Legal Notebooks 1841-1885, Book 9, Folder 64, October 1875. (Property of the Massachusetts Historical Society)

The Writings of Herman Melville, Correspondence, edited by Lynn Horth, Northwestern University Press, Chicago, 1993. P.672 mentions James Colt.

Mass.gov "Associate Justice James D. Colt Memorial"

The Springfield Republican August 19th, 1881. James Colt obituary is on p. 8. The September 13th, 1881 edition has a story on Colt on p. 5. The August 10th, 1881 edition has a three-page story on Colt's suicide, starting on p. 1. The August 11th, 1881 edition has a story on Colt on p. 4.

Bioguide.congress.gov "Train, Charles Russell, 1817-1885"

History.house.gov "Train, Charles Russell"

The Fitchburg Sentinel August 3rd, 1885. Funeral and obituary of Charles Train on p. 3.

The Worcester of 1898: Fifty Years a City, edited by Franklin P. Rice. F.S. Blanchard & Company, Worcester, 1899. (Profiles of HB Staples and ABR Sprague)

History of the Judiciary of Massachusetts, William Thomas Davis. Boston Book Company, 1900. p. 260-1 has profile of Hamilton Staples.

The Worcester Magazine August 1902. Profile of John Hopkins on p. 45-9.

The Boston Post, May 20th, 1902, p.1 story on John Hopkins.

The Boston Post, March 26th, 1891, p.2 story on John Hopkins.

The Springfield Republican, May 20th, 1902, obituary for John Hopkins on p. 12. The June 16th, 1902 edition has a lengthy tribute to John Hopkins on p. 6.

Harvard College Class of 1869 Tenth Report, Riverside Press, Cambridge, MA, 1908. P. 10-15 profile of George Homer Ball.

Harvard College Class of 1869 Thirteenth Report, p. 16-22 on G.H. Ball.

History of Worcester, Massachusetts from its Earliest Settlement, William Lincoln, Charles Hersey Publishing, Worcester. P. 350 has story on G.H. Ball.

Collections of the Worcester Society of Antiquity vol. IX, Published by the Society, Worcester, MA, 1891. p.163-166. Profile of J. Henry Hill has information on both Devens and Ball.

The Springfield Republican, March 27th, 1904. p. 6 has G.H. Ball obituary.

The Worcester Magazine vol. XII, Jan-Dec, 1910, Blanchard Press, Worcester, MA. P. 160-1 has a profile of A.B.R. Sprague.

The Worcester of 1898: Fifty Years a City, edited by Franklin P. Rice. F.S. Blanchard & Company, Worcester, 1899. Profile of A.B.R. Sprague on p. 752-54.

United States Congressional Set, issue 4916 vol. 8, Government Printing Office, 1906. p. 94 has a Sprague profile.

The Fitchburg Sentinel, June 10th, 1903, p. 6 has an obituary of Sheriff Bothwell.

The Springfield Republican, June 10th, 1903, p. 12 has an obituary for Bothwell.

The Springfield Republican, October 20th, 1908, p. 14 has an obituary for Pliny Babbitt.

Report of the Joint Special Committee of the General Court of the Revision of the Public Statutes of the Commonwealth 1881, Rand, Avery, and

Company Press, 1881. p.834 has the 1870 statute on spouses' testifying. *The History of Petersham, Massachusetts, Incorporated April 20, 1754*, by Mabel Coolidge, Petersham Historical Society, 1948. P.258 has Frost story.

Old Landmarks and Historic Spots of Worcester, Massachusetts, John Pearl Spears, Commonwealth Press, Worcester, 1931.

New England Today, "The Curious Case of Asa Snow", by Bethany Bourgault, September 6th, 2016.

Strange Tales From Old Quabbin, J.R. Greene. Highland Press, Athol, MA, 1993. p. 113-6 is on Asa Snow, 117-126 on Samuel J. Frost.

www.ingramcontent.com/pod-product-compliance
Lightning Source LLC
Chambersburg PA
CBHW052128270326
41930CB00012B/2807